KU-619-987

# Science 7–11

Developing primary teaching skills

Clive Carré and Carrie Ovens

London and New York

First published 1994
by Routledge
11 New Fetter Lane, London EC4P 4EE

Simultaneously published in the USA and Canada
by Routledge
29 West 35th Street, New York, NY 10001

© 1994 Clive Carré and Carrie Ovens

Typeset in Palatino by Solidus (Bristol) Limited
Printed and bound in Great Britain by
Clays Ltd, St Ives PLC

All rights reserved. No part of this book may be reprinted or
reproduced or utilized in any form or by any electronic,
mechanical, or other means, now known or hereafter
invented, including photocopying and recording, or in any
information storage or retrieval system, without permission in
writing from the publishers.

*British Library Cataloguing in Publication Data*
A catalogue record for this book is available from the British Library

*Library of Congress Cataloging in Publication Data*
A catalogue record for this book has been requested

ISBN 0-415-10509-9

# Science 7–11

As one of the core areas of the curriculum, science provides particular challenges, especially to teachers working at the top end of the primary age range. Clive Carré and Carrie Ovens, both experienced primary teachers themselves, ask what teachers really need to know, both about their subject and about their children in order to teach science effectively. They give practical guidance on curriculum planning, on balancing enquiry approaches to learning with more formal 'telling' and on the difficult area of collecting and interpreting evidence of children's progress for assessment.

**Clive Carré** has taught in both primary and secondary schools and was coordinator of the Leverhulme Primary Project based at the University of Exeter, where he was senior lecturer in the school of education, prior to his recent retirement. His publications include *Learning to Teach* (Routledge 1993) which he co-authored with Neville Bennett and *Visual Communication in Science* (Cambridge University Press 1985) with David Barlex. **Carrie Ovens** has taught in a number of primary schools as a class teacher and, more recently, as an advisory teacher. She is currently lecturer in education at the University of Exeter.

LIVERPOOL JMU LIBRARY

3 1111 00674 8147

## Curriculum in primary practice series
General editor: Clive Carré

The Curriculum in primary practice series is aimed at students and qualified teachers looking to improve their practice within the context of the National Curriculum. The large format, easy to use texts are interactive, encouraging teachers to engage in professional development as they read. Each contains:

- Summaries of essential research
- Transcripts of classroom interactions for analysis and discussion
- Activities for individual and group use

While all primary teachers will find these books useful, they are designed with the needs of teachers of the 7 to 11 age group particularly in mind.

**Other titles include:**

*Religious education 7–11*
Terence Copley

*Music 7–11*
Sarah Hennessy

**Forthcoming titles in this series in 1995:**

*English 7–11*
David Wray

# Contents

# Figures and tables

**FIGURES**

## TABLES

# Acknowledgements

The writing of this book would not have been possible without the help we have received from the many teachers with whom we have worked over the past few years. Their suggestions and innovatory ideas have helped us to re-focus our own thinking and improve on the activities in the text. We would particularly like to thank Linda Parker, Bickleigh-on-Exe Primary School and Lynne Carré, Alphington Combined School, for their help. We are indebted to the children whose talk and writings gave us and their teachers food for thought; in particular we are grateful to Sam and Clare.

We are indebted to BBC School's Radio and Fred Harris, for Figure 2.5 'The Daily Fib', from *Science Games*, Teachers' Notes, summer 1985. We also thank the following publishers for permission to reprint figures and illustrations: Ginn & Company Ltd for Figure 2.6a, from *Flowering Plants*; Stanley Thornes (Publishers) Ltd for Figure 2.6b, from *Physics for You*; Thomas Nelson, for Figure 2.6c, from *Investigating Materials*, and for Figure 2.6e, from *Discovering Connections*; The Open University Press, for Figure 4.3, from *Words, Science and Learning*; and Simon & Schuster, for Figure 4.4, from *Exploration: A Way of Learning Science*.

Finally we wish to thank our respective spouses, Lynne and Edric for their professional support, sensitive comments and constructive criticism.

# Introduction

There are two myths in teaching that are commonly heard. Some say that teachers need sound academic subject knowledge and can learn about children in the process of teaching them. Others say that the crux of teaching is to understand children, the subject knowledge will come through teaching it. Current thinking is that each of the two views is partially right; as Mary Kennedy succinctly argues:

> Academic subjects and diverse learners are the yin and yang of teaching – opposing and complementary forces ... An erudite portrayal of an important concept has no value if students can't understand it, but neither does an engaging portrayal that is inaccurate.
>
> (Kennedy, 1991)

At no other time has the science curriculum been subjected to such critical scrutiny. The establishment of the National Curriculum with science as a core element was one result of this. The demands made upon primary teachers have consequently altered. In line with the strenuous efforts which have been made to support and promote primary science, particularly to alter its image of being synonymous with nature study, this book offers guidance on teaching science to children from 7 to 11 years old. It cannot be a comprehensive guide, neither can it deal with all subject topics; but it selectively examines instances of effective teaching. Our aim is to help you enhance your practice, by capitalising on what you already know about teaching in general and about children. We hope that the practical suggestions and examples of classroom work will enable you to compare what you do with our perceptions of teaching science at this age level.

Throughout, we have urged a teaching strategy which includes finding out children's intuitive understandings as a start to 'doing science'. We suggest planning activities which challenge their thinking, introduce them to correct vocabulary, and encourage them towards consensus views of adult science. We believe that at times it is appropriate to use 'jam-jar' technology; at other times it is better to use more sophisticated apparatus, chosen specifically to help children understand a concept.

In the same way that there is no *one* scientific method for practising scientists, there is no one way to teach science to primary children. Activities will vary and the strategies you use in teaching will depend on your purpose. There is a need to be flexible, so we have throughout stressed the effective teacher as one who can judiciously *balance* a variety of teaching strategies. Teaching cannot be based entirely on enquiry, nor be completely didactic: it is equally important for children to learn to observe and conduct an investigation, as it is to follow a teacher's argument or watch a demonstration. We know that a great deal of what we know as adults is not derived from direct experiences. So, although we stress the importance of 'hands on' experiences, we suggest that children can and do learn from listening, from media and from handling second hand evidence.

A further balancing act to which we have referred is that of teacher control versus pupil 'empowerment'. The importance of moderating control is that *at times* children should feel that they are responsible for their own learning. This principle of balance fits well the recommendations of the Alexander Report (1992) to which we make reference. Reviewing your practice may call for a more calculated look at your classroom – a systematic approach to put the familiar into a different perspective. We invite you to do so, to check your own science knowledge base for teaching, against a background of current informed opinion and research findings.

The book is organised into the following six sections:

- Unit 1 is essentially about the knowledge that is required to be an effective primary teacher of science, and the components of that knowledge base.
- Unit 2 focuses on the ways teachers explain science to primary children, the various forms that are used as instructional representations to aid learning.
- Unit 3 is about the importance of recognising the misconceptions children may have and the way teachers can use different teaching strategies to help them shift their thinking. It reports a case study on the teaching of forces and energy.
- Unit 4 deals with progression at different levels; how children's understanding can be enhanced through careful yet flexible planning.
- Unit 5 takes assessment as its central theme. It examines different ways of obtaining feedback of understanding from children and provides an insight into the ways they respond by giving their own representations of understanding.
- Unit 6 discusses how teachers' attitudes are an important part of the knowledge base for teaching. Attitudes to the teaching of science and to the nature of science are examined, and invitations to re-evaluate them are provided in the activities.

## DIFFERENT WAYS OF USING THIS BOOK

### For teachers working on their own

You may decide to read the text as a book and increase your own understanding through the ideas and illustrative examples. Trying out the suggested activities with your class will help you challenge your own assumptions about how you teach science. However, there is great benefit from discussing what you do and the outcomes of your class's efforts with your colleagues, informally, or as an organised group activity. There is nothing more beneficial to a school than a feeling that everyone is working to improve professional competence.


**For inservice and professional studies courses**

The text and suggested activities together form an obvious focus for group discussion. Individuals can try out practical activities in their own classrooms. Children's work or transcripts in the text can then be supplemented by your own examples – so much better for comparison because you know the context and the children concerned.

A study group can read a chapter in preparation for a meeting, and illustrate their understanding of it by collecting material (scripts, personal thoughts, tape recordings etc.). Sharing the efforts of your class is an effective way to see how others help their children learn, how imaginative ideas can be 'put across' and the different ways the National Curriculum can be interpreted.

Units vary in length. It is possible to use the text and associated activities in a flexible way, to provide material for sessions of about 1 to 1½ hours. Follow-up discussions on work collected in class can easily take a further 1½ hours. The following symbols are used throughout the book to denote:

    quotations from published materials

    activities

    transcripts of children and/or teachers talking


Clive Carré
Carrie Ovens

Unit 1

# A science knowledge base for teaching

What does it mean to be a competent primary science teacher? The question is not easy to answer, since we know very little about the differences between effective beginning teachers and effective experienced teachers. In attempting an answer we can look at the current debate on the professional development of teachers, which places a considerable emphasis on a teacher's knowledge. An assumption exists that there is a connection between what teachers know and how well they perform in class. If that knowledge could be defined, then the processes of training student-teachers and providing in-service experience would be easier and more effective. What is this 'knowledge base' that teachers are supposed to have to teach effectively?

In proposing a knowledge base for teaching all subjects, Shulman (1986), and others, mainly from the USA, have claimed the central importance of:

1.  Content knowledge, (of facts and concepts), and methods of enquiry.
2.  Making content knowledge comprehensible to learners; knowing about pupils' understandings and misconceptions; knowing about curricular materials.

The most important finding from research developed from Shulman's ideas, in all subjects, is that a teacher's role emerges from an understanding of both subject knowledge and the ways children learn. However, teaching science is different from teaching other subjects; for example, science lessons have a less flexible set of instructional pathways than other disciplines, which means that the sequence of events is more predictable. Further, one major research finding (Stodolski, 1988), shows beyond a doubt that individual teachers do not have one instructional approach all day long; the nature of the subject *shapes* the way a teacher teaches. What does the 'nature of the subject' mean in science? The kinds of knowledge which are likely to shape the way we teach will include, knowledge about science facts and concepts, about enquiry, and about the nature of science. (Refer to Unit 6 for discussion of the latter.)

## SCIENCE CONTENT KNOWLEDGE

Besides the nature of the subject, the National Curriculum (DES, 1989 and 1991) has also helped to shape the way science is taught; by clearly defining the *first* part of the knowledge base for teachers. What it doesn't offer is guidance on the second part: the ways for teachers to help children come to grips with ideas, extend their thinking, weigh evidence, solve problems that matter to them, and so on. It appears that only the integrity of science is acknowledged and not the integrity of the children as scientific thinkers. How do teachers manage the central task of making this vital connection between the various strands of science knowledge and their assortment of learners? By way of example, this is how one young teacher taught a lesson on time and night and day.

After viewing a video film, he discussed ways of telling the time. The children talked about the pendulum, atomic clocks, sand, candle and water clocks and sundials which they had seen on the film. He listened carefully to what the children had to say, and then helped them to make sense of their intuitive ideas, as this extract shows:

|  |  |  |
|---|---|---|
| T. | *So how does the sundial actually work using the Sun? Mark?* |
| Mark. | *When the Sun moves, it's moving the shadow that's on the sundial, down to the triangle.* |
| T. | *It's the shadow of the triangle that moves around the clock. Now Mark said that the shadow moves because the Sun moves. Is that right? Does the Sun actually move across the sky?* |
| Chris. | *Yes. No. Yes. Yes it does.* |
| T. | *You think the Sun moves around the earth do you?* |
| Chris. | *Yes. Yes.* |
| T. | *I don't think so. If you imagine that Vicky's pencil case is the Sun and this is the Earth. Where's Britain? There we are. Now if the Sun was up here, what happens to the Earth during the day? Vicky?* |
| Vicky. | *The Earth moves round.* |
| T. | *That's right.* |

The teacher's demonstration, together with his questioning technique, helped to dispel a common misconception. (Many adults think that the Sun rises in the east and sets in the west, rather than appreciating that this is an *apparent* movement. See Glossary under 'alternative frameworks'.)

A little later the teacher placed imaginary children on a globe, and asked questions about when they would see dawn, and so on. Some were confused, so he used an analogy to explain the rotation of the Earth and its effect on night and day:

T.   *Has anyone ever been on a merry-go-round at the fair? . . . If you have a friend standing watching you, you can imagine your friend's the Sun, because he stays still. And this merry-go-round you can imagine is the earth spinning around and around. When you can't see your friend on the ground, then you can imagine that that is night time. When you're sitting on this thing that goes round and round, to you the whole fairground seems to be moving, doesn't it? But it isn't really. It's still, because you're the one that's*

*moving. And all of us on this earth are moving around as if we are on a big wheel at the fair, and the Sun is standing still in the sky.*

He was sufficiently competent in his content knowledge to ask appropriate questions and provide spontaneous, simple representations to explain a difficult idea. Activity 1.1 enquires into a small part of your science content understanding.

 ACTIVITY 1.1  UNDERSTANDING BASIC ASTRONOMY

### Analysis of transcripts

Look carefully at the two lesson segments. In what ways do you think the teacher's subject knowledge helped his pupils' understanding?
Which part of his explanation may have caused confusion?

### Test yourself

Which of the following statements are true? (Answers at end of this unit.)

1.  The Earth orbits the sun every 24 hours.
2.  The Moon is one of the nine planets.
3.  The Moon is held in its orbit round the Earth by the gravitational pull of the Earth.
4.  Our Sun is a star.
5.  Planets move but stars are stationary.
6.  The daily rotation of the Earth causes night and day.
7.  The Moon produces its own light, but less than the Sun.

Testing your understanding in the very first activity is to stress a very important point. We are all 'mixed ability' and our opportunities to learn science have been varied. That places the recent research on teachers' lack of understanding in perspective. Recent research, for example, (Mant and Summers, 1993) shows that primary teachers have unscientific ideas about astronomy. In other areas too researchers have shown primary teachers to have similar misconceptions to their pupils.

The level at which primary teachers need to understand science in order to teach it is a contentious issue. There is no clear answer to what would count as an 'adequate understanding of science', but there is a basic assumption that it should be adequate to teach children competently to appropriate levels in the National Curriculum. Regardless of one's lack of background in science, there is pressure to come to grips with content knowledge. For example, a report by Her Majesty's Inspectorate (HMI) in 1989 on primary science indicated that, 'in taking steps to ensure that practical work is given sufficient attention, many tend to emphasise the acquisition of skills at the expense of scientific knowledge and understanding. This imbalance needs to be corrected'. Why is knowledge of science facts and concepts so important?

The findings from the Leverhulme Primary Project, (Bennett and Carré 1993) based on student-teachers' understanding of science, showed that those with *higher* levels of content knowledge and knowledge of process skills in science showed particular patterns of effective science teaching:

- They planned in detail organisational matters and provided appropriate activities for children to make sense of science.
- Their presentation at the beginning of the lesson explained its purpose and offered a clear link with the practical work which followed.
- Their teaching approaches were flexible, and included both knowledge-telling and knowledge-transforming methods.
- They were able to generate and use instructional representations.
- They were good listeners, respected children's prior knowledge, and indicated if their responses were correct or inappropriate. They were able to challenge children's ideas and beliefs.

It is the last criterion, about challenging children's statements in science lessons, that frequently causes anxiety, more so than in other areas of the curriculum. Symington and Osborne (1985) pointed out that experienced teachers, confident in handling other activities, behave as inexperienced teachers when teaching science. The concern is to ensure that a teacher will have sufficient knowledge to see when a pupil's response is in conflict with adult scientific views, and do something about it. Activity 1.2 will give you an idea of the way you might challenge children's ideas, and then help them further their understanding.

 ACTIVITY 1.2  CONFLICTING IDEAS?

Imagine you were the teacher of the children in the following case studies. How would you have responded to them?

Case 1: A group of 7 year olds are observing ice-cubes melting in water.

|  |  |
|---|---|
| T. | *What a mystery! It's gone. Where do you think its gone?* |
| Sean. | *Its gone up into the sky and into the clouds.* |
| T. | *Really? There's no clouds in here.* |
| Nathan. | *Because the water's cold and it melted.* |

Case 2: A group of 9 to 10 year olds are being introduced to the concept of density. The teacher poured equal quantities of oil and water into a jar, shook it and left the contents to settle.

|  |  |
|---|---|
| T. | *Listen, the oil goes above the water, even though we put the oil in before the water. Now, why do you think that is? Why do you think the oil goes above the water?* |
| Jane. | *Because the water's heavier than the oil?* |

Case 3: A teacher has been talking to a class of 10 year olds about the classification of rocks. After watching a TV programme about volcanoes, the children were engaged in discussion about the origin of types of rocks.

T.  *Sedimentary rocks are usually, but not always, found in layers, where sediments like sand and mud have been laid on top of each other and then become compacted and changed into rock over a very long time.*

Joshua.  *A volcano is sedimentary because it has layers of lava around the outside.*

Symington and Osborne suggest that the main problem with teachers feeling 'inexperienced' in science was one of over concern about 'correctness', and too little concern with children's existing understandings. What does this mean in everyday teaching?

One student-teacher started her lesson by asking a class of 11 year olds, 'Now can anybody tell me what a force is?' Her *intention* at the beginning of the lesson was to find out what was in their heads. Their answers included, 'Force of when you kick something, you use power' and 'when you force a door open'. The teacher accepted the statements without exploring what the children meant by these phrases. She didn't want to discuss it in front of the whole class, and in her eagerness to get started with practical work she didn't let the pupils explain their experiences about everyday forces. What she *did* tell them, quickly, was that forces act on the cars they were about to test, so causing a change in their motion. She also mentioned that toy cars run down slopes because they are acted upon by a force called gravity.

It is significant that she gave no attention to what the children thought, in her scramble to put over scientifically correct ideas. Yet what children understand, as opposed to what teachers think they understand, has received considerable international attention and has been the focus of a large body of research. The message from researchers is that children's misconceptions in science cannot be ignored, they need to be explored. One way to do this is to set conditions for 'conceptual change' teaching, and this is addressed in Unit 3.

## PROCESS SKILLS

The National Curriculum makes it quite clear that school science activity is about doing and thinking; first hand experiences which encourage children to observe, carry out investigations and interpret what they have found out. At Key Stage 2 (i.e. 7 to 11 years old.) the process skill element has a weighting of 50 per cent. In other words, activities should aim to develop the skill element and the concepts in tandem; they are totally interdependent. Both have to be addressed whether one is teaching thematically (e.g. a topic on 'Change') or treating a concept area such as 'electricity' as a discrete unit of learning. It is the method of enquiry, using process skills, which distinguishes science most clearly from other subjects. However, the notion of being able to test a hypothesis by fair-testing, to evaluate evidence and to replicate results are not easy concepts for children to grasp.

Wynne Harlen (1985) emphasises the dual nature of science, being a set of ideas and a method, and points to the implications of introducing primary children to science. She says:

(children) will be developing ideas about the world around from their earliest years. If these ideas are based on casual observation, non-investigated events and the acceptance of hearsay, then they are likely to be non-scientific, 'everyday' ideas ... children's science education should make children want to do just that (put ideas to the test) and should provide them with the skills to do it. Then they not only have the chance to modify their ideas, but they learn to be skeptical about so-called 'truths'.

It could therefore be argued that the most important reason for accepting science as a core subject is that it provides children with a means of checking everyday ideas. However some would argue that those 'skills' which Harlen talks about, those which enable children to make sense of their lives and to challenge critically their experiences, may not need to be taught.

 ### ACTIVITY 1.3  A 3 YEAR OLD INVESTIGATES

Sam had discovered that if he pushed a swivel-chair hard enough it would rotate for quite a number of turns. This kept him busy for a while until he decided to put his box of crayons onto the chair. He placed it in the centre of the seat and pushed very hard. His face showed amazement as he noticed that the crayons did not move. In silence he took out a few crayons and placed them next to the box. As he rotated the chair the loose crayons slid off, but the box remained. He grinned, tipped all the crayons onto the chair and threw away the box. With one big push the crayons were scattered around the room. His face showed just how pleased he was of his achievement.

What elements of the science process can you infer from this child's investigation? How might you explain to an 11 year old the forces operating on the box and the crayons?

Claxton (1986) argues that there is no need to *teach* children process skills; it is insulting to children's intelligence to suggest that they need to be told how to observe, measure, hypothesise and so on:

 it could be argued that children are already expert at these skills, having been practising them all their lives; that their expertise is none the worse for being intuitive rather than explicit, articulate and logical; that there is no evidence that any training of such general capabilities either occurs in science lessons, or, if it does, that it transfers to anywhere else; that the psychological evidence suggests that such transfer will not occur.

It is easy to empathise with Claxton's view. Children are very good at using all their senses, as the examples in this book testify, and the evidence for transfer of process skills is not at all convincing. What *is* generally acknowledged is that 'doing' practical work, and then reflecting about it through talking and writing, are the means by which children make most sense of science. In the following units the way teachers integrate general process skills into their teaching, and the unique role of scientific investigation will be explored. However it is the intention in this unit to raise certain methodological issues through examining three process skills: *observing*, although common to many subjects, subsumes others in science, like classifying and measuring. *Hypothesising* and *investigating* are process skills characteristically scientific, even though other subjects do use the terms.

## Observing

Observing is not unique to science contexts. We have all experienced in childhood the fascination of being totally captivated with observing an object or an event; in an essentially personal way we weave a cloak of meaning that incorporates our experiences and imagination.

Unfortunately in the classroom the mental imagery is not always what the teacher is expecting. For example, children supposed to be examining the structure of a flower, because they have been told to do so, may be more involved in the most acute observations of the antics of aphids on the stem!

Many adults if asked to observe a burning candle would mention the colours of the flame, but how many would consider including the smell of the wax vapour as children often do? At times children's observations are richer and more complex than their later, more controlled responses. So whereas adults screen for relevance and discard those common-place associations of ideas, derived from convention or social usage, children are at the mercy of many alternative viewpoints. In making sense of what they observe, often using wild categories of their own making, they give statements which are at times difficult to interpret, or laughable in their inappropriateness or illogical reasoning.

Children are quite capable of picking out the most minute details, but require guidance in detecting the relevant and discarding the irrelevant. Research findings on children's capabilities in science skills can be misleading and results should be interpreted with caution.

For example, in the surveys between 1980 and 1984, the Assessment of Performance Unit (APU) gave practical observation tests to 10 to 11 year olds. Some of the results (DES, 1983) indicated that children were concerned with gross features rather than more detailed ones, but were able to see details when asked to give attention to them. Also they were better in noticing differences than similarities. The APU acknowledge that these results depend very much on the child's reaction to context; away from the test, children can be helped to observe similarities, differences and details when the purpose is made clear to them.

For example, having taken her 7 year olds to a butterfly farm, the teacher asked the children to list the *similarities* between moths and butterflies. One list included: 'Both got antennae, Both got tongues, Both lay eggs, They both got balls on top of their antennae, Both have wings.' The teacher didn't 'correct' the lists the children produced. Instead she asked everyone in class to make a paper model of the head of a moth and butterfly. She said that, 'craft work required that they added to their first hand observations by looking for information and pictures in books'. In this way the teacher encouraged more effective observation.

The same class had collected common caterpillars and were responsible for feeding them. One group set off, identification books in hand, to gather food. Observations needed to sort the various leaves, using a key, were not easy, but the 'real-life' necessity made the observations particularly acute!

| | |
|---|---|
| Rosina. | *No, we're looking for dock leaves – not that shape. Look (pointing in the book) there's a pointy end here!* |
| Shaun. | *But none of them look like that. What about this one? It's got a long thing here.* |
| Samantha. | *No, you don't want to kill the caterpillars – if they eat that they'll die.* |
| Shaun. | *If they don't like the smell of it they won't eat it – animals aren't stupid you know.* |

Which perhaps might have led to an investigation, but didn't! The context provided an opportunity for these children to use their considerable powers of observation to cope with a difficult key. Similarly, children might be encouraged to report back their everyday observations, those in which they are genuinely involved: from television programmes (weather maps, nature programmes, *Tomorrow's World*), from data (advertising, bill-boards, graphs and tables in magazines), from instrument scales (thermometers, radio dials, recorder panels) from reading and all the minutiae associated with their hobbies.

## Hypothesising

One important aspect of thinking in investigations is, as the National Curriculum states, to 'formulate testable hypotheses', a translation for younger children being the equally cumbersome 'suggesting tentative explanations'. It is recognised as an important process skill, for it has a central role in developing children's ability to *explain* observations or relationships. This is no easy matter for the child to accomplish or the teacher to assess. The imprecise way children use language in this context makes it very difficult to judge whether or not they have mastered the skill.

Swatton (1992) looked at 11 year olds' attempts to hypothesise. The investigation, which he demonstrated, concerned the rate of absorption of ink onto chromatography paper. He then gave them the results from another group of children (Table 1.1).

*Table 1.1.* Children's results from the chromatography investigation

| Amount of ink in cubic centimetres | How far it spread in centimetres |
|---|---|
| 1 | 3 |
| 2 | 4.5 |
| 3 | 7 |
| 4 | 10 |
| 5 | 15 |

From observing these results they were asked what problem the children were investigating. Here are two of their responses:

Pupil A.   To see whether the amount of ink affects how far it spreads.
Pupil B.   They were investigating how much further the ink spread, depending on the amount of ink.

As Swatton points out, pupils A and B have clearly linked the two variables in a form which would allow the relationship to be tested by systematic investigation. Other responses selected from this research are in Activity 1.4.

 **ACTIVITY 1.4  CAN CHILDREN FORMULATE TESTABLE HYPOTHESES?**

What degree of confidence would you have in stating that the children's responses below indicate whether or not they have been able to describe the original hypothesis, developed by the other group of children?

1. They were seeing if the amount would change the spread.
2. The children were trying to find out how far each amount of ink spreads.
3. They were investigating how far the ink could spread around and investigating the amount of ink.
4. The children were investigating how far the ink spreads and the amount of cubic centimetres.
5. How far a certain amount of ink spreads.
6. How far it spreads.
7. The amount of ink.
8. Whether different amounts of ink made any difference.
9. How the ink travels – how fast or slow.
10. I think they were trying to measure the ink.

In making your decision you may wish to consider the way the child has used language to express the hypothesis and the way they have referred to the variables.

Helping children to formulate testable hypotheses is no easy task. One teacher does so by guiding them to convert their question into a statement, and placing it as a large heading to a display, so that it can be referred to during the investigation. The statement is in the form of the 'if ... then ...' logic, which helps to direct children's attention towards the variables in the investigation. Two examples show her prominent display headings, the first in the context of water and transportation, and the second where the testable question was, 'In what ways can we increase the size of bubbles?'

> **If** we drip water onto the pile of gravel in the gutter **Then** the finer bits will come away first in the stream.
> **If** we increase the concentration of washing-up liquid **Then** the bubbles will get bigger.

The next example is less sophisticated. This teacher encouraged her children to ask lots of questions, rather than make statements. Notice how this example illustrates not only how children of 7 years old hypothesised, but how the creation of hypotheses was based on previous understanding. Two girls were investigating the way different wooden shapes slid down a ramp. Their previous knowledge about things sliding or rolling was felt to be important by the teacher, and so predictions were made before the test. Natasha offered a hypothesis, 'I think the shapes with rounded ends will roll better.' Her hypothesis led the group to set up an investigation to test it. With the teacher's help they decided on the height of the slope, the starting point and the way to release the shapes. Their initial predictions had led them to a successful fair-test; notice the ambiguity in the language they used to record this. In Figure 1.1, 'No Slide' means this shape will not roll (answering the question), it will slide! Her arrows suggest the movement.

**Investigating**

One important teaching skill is to help children use science process skills. How might this be done? The APU (DES, 1988) research findings suggest that teaching process skills in isolation is not as effective as teaching them in the context of an investigation, (with the possible exception of learning about measurement and converting data into graphical form). Here is how one teacher introduced a class of 7 year olds to learning about the procedure of an investigation. He said, 'I wanted to build upon their existing understanding of the concept of fairness, from their everyday experiences of playing games. Most children are aware that rules are needed to be fair, so the games I provided helped the children to reflect on what was happening, and helped them to recognise the variables in a simple way.' In the first game the question posed to the class was, 'Who is the fastest grabber of Smarties?' Much talk was needed to decide what was meant by 'the fastest'. Eventually a testable question was put on the board: Which person can get the Smartie off the table first?

The game was played with the teacher at one end of the table and one child at the other. The teacher, with mock seriousness, cheated outrageously: by placing the Smartie on the table closer to him, by calling out 'Ready, steady, go!' with the timing to his advantage, by standing close to the table and placing the child some distance away, by having his hands closer to the Smartie than the child, and so on. The indignant cries of the children demanded that rules be invented. Everyone wrote down their list to ensure fairness. Chloe wrote her suggestions on the computer (Figure 1.2), and her understanding at 7 years old, about the impossibility of ever achieving absolute fairness in an investigation is remarkable.

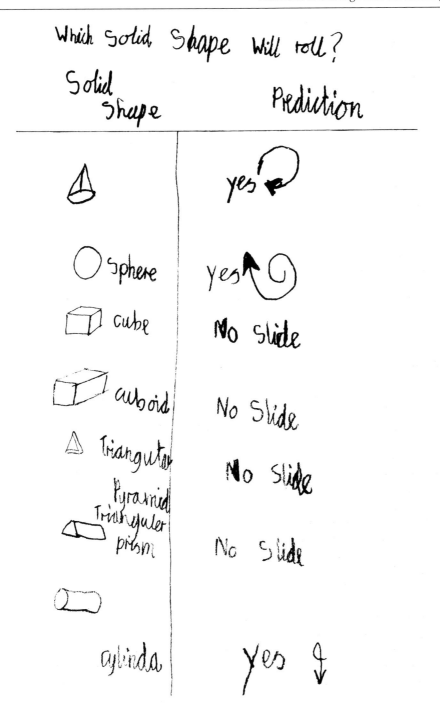

*Figure 1.1*  Children's predictions about wooden shapes sliding

---

*The fastest Smartie grabber.*

The rules are, you must have two people. Put a Smartie in the middle of the table and say ready steady go. But you must not touch the people or the Smartie. The one that gets the Smartie first is the winner. It would be a good idea if the people were twins and then everything would be the same, the same height, length of arms and things like that.

Chloe.

---

*Figure 1.2* Rules to be the fastest Smartie grabber

For older children much practice and talking through ideas about variables is necessary; about how decisions are made on what to measure, and the best way to measure the dependent variable (i.e. the outcome). The need to encourage children to be critical of their investigation is therefore vital, yet in practice evaluation is often the last thing children want to do. They are so pleased with their achievement.

In the above example, for older children, it would be necessary to explain that, 'who grabs it first' is the outcome of the investigation, the thing of interest to the investigator and needs to be measured, (the dependent variable). This will alter depending on the people taking part, (the independent variable) who are changed systematically. Everyone in the class takes part so that a comparison can be made. For this investigation to be fair, certain conditions had to be controlled as well as possible (the control variables). It was this third element which the 7 year olds in the example above were particularly good at!

Teachers adopt different routines to help children become familiar and confident in understanding scientific methods, and the importance of fair-testing. A teacher of 11 year olds has this reminder on permanent display:

---

The variables in an investigation that need to be identified are:

- The independent variables, those to be *changed*.
- The dependent variables, those to be *observed or measured*.
- The control variables, those to be kept the *same* for 'a fair-test'.

---

Based on this she produces sheets for the children to plan their investigations. The following questions, on the sheet, guide their thinking:

- What's your investigable question?
- What will you observe or measure? (dependent variable)
- What will you choose to change? (independent variable)
- What will you keep the same? (control variable)
- How will your results be used to answer the question?

In any progression it is wise to introduce a simple investigation of the 'Smartie grabber' kind, where measurement is simple – they either grab it or they don't. More demanding investigations enable children to measure the dependent variable when it is continuous, like the height a ball bounces or the weight needed to bend a model bridge. (See Unit 4 for investigations with parachutes.)

## DIFFERENT FORMS OF SCIENCE ACTIVITY

Science activity does not always mean investigating. For example, some activities depend on careful observation, 'where is the Moon on successive nights?' or 'how many different plants grow in our lawn?'. These do not involve fair-testing and procedures for identifying variables; the children are not investigating. Part of the research programme in the Leverhulme Primary Project (Bennett and Carré, 1993) was to observe student-teachers and newly qualified teachers teaching science. In Unit 3, Activity 3.3 illustrates some of the many forms of science activity observed, from using secondary sources to investigations. It is certainly not a comprehensive list, but gives examples of the ways student-teachers translated the programmes of study of the National Curriculum into teaching strategies. By consciously planning a variety of activities, with different purposes in mind, a wide range of assessment objectives and science investigations can be achieved.

Another point worth mentioning is that in any activity the *degree of intervention* in children's learning can be altered: a considerable amount of help can be given via a worksheet, or minimal guidance can be given in an open ended investigation. A dilemma in planning is whether to 'play safe', and adopt routines within a tight teacher framework, or to plan open tasks, where pupils are invited to ask their own questions and test their own hypotheses. The open task may be judged by the children as a *high risk*, i.e. one where the intellectual demand is too great. Alternatively they may see the task as *too ambiguous*, i.e. not enough help in how to proceed and how it will be marked. The way children perceive a task will affect the way they respond; some children adopt strategies to reduce both risk and ambiguity, asking for more and more help. Who wants to spend time thinking about problem-solving, when with a little whining the teacher will provide a solution?

Decisions about activities are therefore important, not only for planning, but for diagnosing errors and for making judgments about assessment, (see further discussion in Unit 5). Activity 1.5 will focus on helping you get an appropriate balance.

ACTIVITY 1.5  BALANCING A RANGE OF ACTIVITIES

Select one content area of your own choosing and plan a suitable range of science activities over a period of six weeks. In making decisions about the nature of the activities, have in mind:

1.  Tight structure (*cage*) or open (loose-*frame*work) tasks; the *cage–frame* dimension of activity management. How closed or open should the tasks be? How much risk? How much empowerment for the children?
2.  That listening is an active process and not passive, as once thought (see *The Bullock Report*, DES, 1975). Adopting a 'telling' strategy is perfectly legitimate: when explaining, modelling a procedure or demonstrating a piece of apparatus.
3.  Part investigations are at times more desirable than whole investigations; for example, helping children with data collection, interpreting results to find patterns, *reading* information from tables, charts and graphs and *constructing* graphs of class results.

*Note*: Have a purpose for the activity, so that you can justify your decisions in planning.

**How does one go about getting this knowledge base?**

It is obvious that any one category of the knowledge base is ineffectual without the others. A brilliant exposition of physics is just as useless if taught in chaos, as a well controlled lesson in which no science is learned. Attention needs to be focussed as much on the subject as on pedagogy. A newly qualified teacher is very likely to be asked to teach a topic never previously learned, at the same time as having to learn the skills of the classroom. There isn't a right way to go about getting this knowledge. Most teachers want people to help them, and gain most benefit from discussing with other teachers, the science coordinator, a spouse or friend. Others find it helpful to refer to specialised texts or read science texts used by secondary pupils, e.g. Johnson, K. (1991) *Physics for You*, Cheltenham: Stanley Thornes; Warren, P. (1988) *Physics for Life*, London: Murray. Especially helpful are those texts which give details of content knowledge and add some pedagogical context and advice, e.g. Jarvis, T. (1991) *Children and Primary Science*, London: Cassell and *The Nuffield Primary Science* series (1993) Glasgow: Collins Educational. Some television programmes provide considerable help by presenting material which a teacher might find difficult to obtain, in exciting and effective ways.

To help teachers learn about the *nature* of science, a comprehensive survey can be found in Chalmers, A. (1982) *What Is This Thing Called Science?* 2nd edn, Milton Keynes: Open University Press. A personal favourite on the subject is the elegantly written *Pluto's Republic*, by Medawar, which is mentioned in Unit 6. For an insight to the processes of science at work and the foundations of our scientific knowledge, *The Search for Solutions* (1980) by Judson, H., London: Hutchinson, provides a beautifully illustrated and readable account.

Human and textual resources help teachers prepare to teach new material; they learn appropriate levels of subject content and are then in a position to devise ways of making that knowledge understandable to the specific learners in their class. This important element of the knowledge base is dealt with in the next unit.

## SUMMARY

For far too long debate has polarised an emphasis on content or process approaches to teaching science. This is simplistic. Although the sections on content knowledge and process skills have been separated in this chapter, both together are necessary in learning activities.

Research indicates the importance of a knowledge base for teaching. Subject content knowledge is important, but not exclusively so; teaching also requires a knowledge of the principles of enquiry, understanding of the nature of science and awareness of how learners develop. Not all science learning is achieved through investigations. Other activities, such as discussing, writing, reading, model making and role play are important too. Practical and non-practical activity play a role in furthering conceptual understanding. Knowing the purpose for an activity is vital. Different forms of investigation play different roles in learning science; some process skills can be taught separately from whole investigations.

## ANSWERS TO ACTIVITY 1.1

Numbers 3, 4 and 6 are true.

Unit 2

# Communicating subject knowledge in the classroom

The previous unit focused on the first part of Lee Shulman's knowledge base for teaching, understanding the content and processes of science. This unit deals with the second category, emphasising the importance of the teacher's role in presenting information and explaining to children.

Teaching children is a highly unpredictable activity and researchers acknowledge that teachers are involved in a multiplicity of tasks; managing classroom groups and individuals, coping with discipline problems, establishing routines, dealing with resources, selecting tasks and assessing. It is against this complex background science is taught. There are two aspects of particular importance.

Evidence indicates that children model themselves on their teachers. The *way* a teacher teaches gives messages about what, for example, enquiry in science is about. But equally important is the repertoire of methods which teachers use to convey to children science content knowledge. Shulman (1986) referred to this ability in terms of its teachability:

 the most useful forms of representation of those (distinctive) ideas, the most powerful analogies, illustrations, examples, explanations and demonstrations – in a word, the ways of representing and formulating the subject that make it comprehensible to others.

These 'forms of representation' are the essence, in Shulman's terms, of teaching an academic subject to learners of different ability. Teachers are constantly transforming content knowledge when they explain. They adapt resources and modify instructional representations for different learners, often without knowing how effective their translation has been!

I.M. MARSH LIBRARY LIVERPOOL L17 6BD
TEL. 0151 231 5216/5299

## HOW CONTENT IS REPRESENTED IN CLASSROOMS

It must first be emphasised that there is no *one* correct way of representing an idea or an event. In Unit 1 a teacher was described, representing in an appropriate way, the movement of the Earth with reference to a merry-go-round. An alternative could have been to use a worksheet, where pupils are invited to look at Lowry life figures on a series of diagrams of the Earth and Sun and predict whether they are in darkness or in light. Choice is personal.

Primary science involves a great deal of 'hands-on' activity. For much of the time teachers arrange tasks where children handle materials: they find the hardness of rock samples, complete circuits on a circuit board, classify a group of flowers and so on. However, science does not *always* dwell in the land of the concrete. Teachers need at times to transform science content for pupils in the form of an abstraction, a representation of the real thing: an infra-red photograph of an insulated house, X-ray sheets of part of the skeleton, a video in time-lapse showing germination, a satellite picture of weather patterns, diagrams illustrating simple genetics, graphical information, and database printouts. At a still higher level of abstraction teachers have to present those concepts dealing with such ideas as: heat, geological time, electrical current, photosynthesis and energy. Newly qualified teachers are disadvantaged. It takes time to develop a bank of instructional representations; those gleaned from ideas in curriculum materials and those created anew. Further, constructing them and working out how to use them in class are not the same thing. It takes time to try out and modify different versions of the same representation, for no two groups of learners are the same.

There is very clear evidence of the relationship between what a teacher knows about science and the way instructional representations are used. McDiarmid and his co-workers (1989) report on the critical influence of subject understanding on the way a subject is made known to pupils. They emphasise the importance of a teacher having a deep understanding of the content matter necessary to represent the concept or procedure, characterising this aspect of a teacher's knowledge base as: 'not simply a repertoire of multiple representations' but rather 'a way of thinking that facilitates the generation of these transformations, the development of "pedagogical *thinking*".' The next activity invites you to to try out some 'pedagogical thinking'.

 ### ACTIVITY 2.1  REPRESENTING THE SAME SCIENTIFIC IDEA IN DIFFERENT WAYS

In Attainment Target 3 (Materials and their properties) pupils should: 'understand the water cycle in terms of the physical processes involved'.

How might you represent this level 5 statement to your class? If possible compare your effort with those of others.

It is helpful to categorise different ways of representing by referring to the theory of instruction of Bruner (1974). He too was concerned with effective sequences of presentation, and distinguished its three *modes*:

A representation of the world or of some segment of one's experience has several interesting features. For one thing, it is in some medium. We may represent some events by the actions they require, by some form of picture, or in words or other symbols. There are many subvarieties within each of the three media – the *enactive*, the *iconic* or the *symbolic*. A representation of an event is selective. In constructing a model of something, we do not include everything about it. The principle of selectivity is usually determined by *the ends to which a representation is put.* (our italics)

In science we create different types of 'models' to explain things: a construction in 'Lego' to show the performance of an object, or abstract symbols to demonstrate a system or a possible theory. At both concrete and abstract levels Bruner emphasises that the model is never complete in every detail. Only those elements *necessary for its purpose* are selected. For example, think of the usefulness of the London Underground map in finding one's way around, yet, as many have pointed out, it is only a representation of the real thing – distances and directions are misrepresented.

In Activity 2.1, you might have used the enactive mode, for example using the steam from a boiling kettle on a pane of glass to demonstrate condensation and so on, or the iconic mode in the form of a blackboard diagram, or a symbolic mode, using words.

In your own experience you will probably have noticed that as young children communicate, enactive and iconic forms predominate; the symbolic modes become increasingly important as they grow older. One can see the intellectual development of children in terms of the successful mastery of the three modes, and with the symbolic mode, language is the prime means. Obviously the modes are not exclusive, and a mix of all three is common when teachers communicate to children, or when they are 're-presenting' knowledge back to the teacher. It is important to note that Bruner (1966) makes a distinction between his theory of learning and theory of instruction (even though learning and instruction are reciprocal processes, and the distinction is often blurred). His ideas about learning are *descriptive*, and he talks of the three ways in which someone 'knows' something; through doing it, through a mental image of it or through some symbolic means, like language. However his theory of instruction is *prescriptive*, his intention being to improve technique, so he suggests that a body of knowledge should be structured, with effective sequences of material.

## CASE STUDIES OF PEDAGOGICAL THINKING

The act of 'putting it over well' involves knowing your science content well enough to enable you to design some form of representation, in a suitable form for the learners.

### ACTIVITY 2.2  JUDGING THE STRENGTHS AND LIMITATIONS OF REPRESENTATIONS

In the examples which follow, Case-studies 1–7, try to judge the *usefulness, appropriateness* and *correctness* of the representations in teaching different science concepts to different aged children.

Consider how you might have taught each case study differently.

**Case 1.** Ref: National Curriculum Attainment Target 4 Strand (i) Level 3 – 'know that a complete circuit is needed for electrical devices to work'.

The photograph in Figure 2.1 shows the teacher explaining to a group of 7 year olds why a complete circuit is needed to light a bulb, and the function of a switch.

> T. *Can you just hold hands in a circle? In a way, what is happening – if I was the battery and I was giving power, it is able to come all the way around because it can pass through us. If I was to take my hand off Joanna's, what have I done?*
>
> Grace. *It would stop it from going round that way.*

*Figure 2.1*  Children discovering the world of electricity

> T.  *Like doing this (unclips the wire from the battery terminal). What has happened now?*
>
> Daniel.  *Power has stopped. It needs two of them.*
>
> T.  *It has to go round in a complete – James has used the word 'circle'. But this circle has been broken . . . If I hold on again what will happen?*
>
> Daniel.  *It'll start again.*

(Linda's account of teaching electricity is given in Parker, 1990.)

*Case 2.* Ref: National Curriculum Attainment Target 3 Strand (i) Level 4 – 'be able to classify materials as solids, liquids and gases on the basis of simple properties which relate to their everyday uses'.

A class of 9 to 10 year olds were studying the effects of weather on soil and rock. Their teacher decided to introduce them to the effect ice has on breaking down rocks. She first gave a dramatic demonstration of the effect of ice expanding, by filling a bottle full of water, fitting in a cork, and leaving in a freezer overnight. The children could see that the ice had taken up more space and pushed the cork out! Her explanation involved teaching about the particulate nature of matter, in a simple way. Using two diagrams of dots, she emphasised that the *same* amount of water took up more space when it was ice than when it was water. The amount of matter was the same in liquid and solid form, but the particles had spread out in the greater volume of ice. The children then discussed the effect of ice forming in cracks in rocks.

(*Note*: The National Curriculum does not require the early teaching of the behaviour of molecules and atoms; however there is an argument for teaching about the particulate nature of matter in a simple way at an early age. It not only provides a fundamental organising framework for teaching science concepts such as heat conduction and behaviour of gases and so on, it introduces the notion of a scientific model as a way of explaining the structure and properties of materials. The DES circular 6/89 indicated that this model was appropriate for some pupils in the second key stage and Leisten, in an article in *The Times Educational Supplement* 23 Oct. 1992, suggests that primary children have the understanding to be able to use it.)

*Case 3.* Ref: National Curriculum Attainment Target 4 Strand (i) Programme of Study – 'They should investigate the properties of magnetic and non-magnetic materials'.

The teacher wanted to help a group of 11 year olds understand that invisible magnetic fields around magnets were three-dimensional. The children had already investigated the effect of a horse-shoe magnet placed on a plastic envelope containing iron-filings (he was aware of the possibility of loose iron-filings damaging the eye). The teacher then demonstrated the three-dimensional effect, using the magnet on a plastic box, as shown in Figure 2.2. The children were then invited to draw the magnetic field using their knowledge from two sets of experiences.

*Case 4.* Ref: National Curriculum Attainment Target 1 Strand (i) Level 2 – 'ask questions such as "how?", "why?" and "what will happen if?", suggest ideas and make predictions'; Strand (ii) Level 4 – 'carry out a fair-test'; and Strand (iii) Level 4 – 'draw conclusions which link patterns in observations to the original prediction'.

*Figure 2.2* Demonstrating the three-dimensional magnetic field of a  horse-shoe magnet

A powerful way to introduce ideas is through narrative. *The Indian in the Cupboard* by Lynne Reid Banks is a delightful story of a boy who is given a plastic Indian for his birthday. It comes alive when it is placed in a small cupboard, and the door is locked, but still remains small. How did it happen?

The teacher of a class of 9 year olds read this part of the story:

> As he had figured this out so far, the cupboard, or the key, or both together, brought plastic things to life, or if they were already alive, turned them into plastic. There were a lot of questions to be answered, though. Did it only work with plastic? Would, say, wooden or metal figures also come to life if shut up in the cupboard? How long did they have to stay in there for the magic to work? Overnight? Or did it happen right away?

The activity which the teacher devised, naturally could not be of a practical nature! What the class enjoyed was being 'adviser' to the boy in the story. The children looked at the features which had to be systematically changed (the independent variable), picked out the dependent variable (judged to be alive or plastic) and considered the various features that had to be kept the same (control variables) if it was to be a fair-test. The task allowed the children to reinforce their understanding from practical work, by considering 'genuine' problems in the imaginative world of fiction.

*Case 5.* Ref: National Curriculum Attainment Target 3 Strand (iv). The programme of study calls for children making observations through fieldwork, about the distribution of rocks and soils, and the evidence for major geological changes.

Although this teacher of 11 year olds had discussed some geological features, in general terms, with layers of different coloured plasticine, she wanted to encourage her class to record evidence for themselves. On a field trip she drew carefully the cliff face from a distance, particularly how the rock banding had been interrupted and sloped, and the shape of the bay, (see Figure 2.3). Her art work acted as a model, which the children had in mind when they produced their own versions. Their drawings became the focus for discussion; how the action of water had affected the shape of the bay, how the rock banding had become interrupted (faulted) and sloped, and which hypotheses could account for the origin of the features they had drawn. The view from a distance was followed by a closer look at the cliff face, to try to match their initial thoughts with their new perspective, to provide an understanding of the geological history of that region.

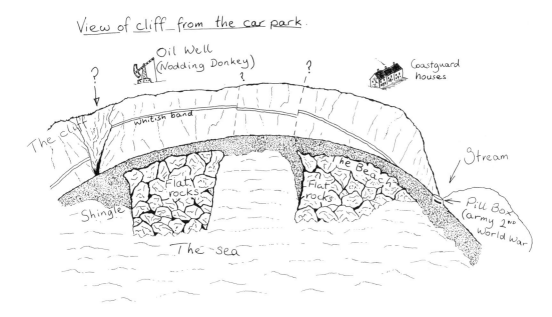

*Figure 2.3* Representing ideas of earth science through drawing

*Case 6.* Ref: National Curriculum Attainment Target 4 Strand (v) – 'They should learn about the motions of the Earth, Moon and Sun in order to explain day and night, day length ... and the seasons.

Previously this class of 11 year olds had looked at various aspects of the solar system. They had considered the apparent movement of the Sun across the sky, and their teacher had used a simple model (football and tennis ball with a spotlight) to explain night and day in terms of the Earth's rotation. They had also found out that one revolution around the Sun represented one year.

During the summer term, the children were studying further aspects of astronomy. They talked about going home in the dark during December and the problems of getting to sleep at night in July. They were well aware of the changing length of daylight. The teacher used the geared model shown in the photograph in Figure 2.4 to explain the length of day and the reasons for the seasons.

T.   *Think back to when you were reading the books, they all mentioned the tilt of the Earth on its axis. With this model we can see clearly what they meant. As I move the Earth, like this rotating around the Sun, focus your attention on the direction the axis is tilting.*

Zoe.   *Oh! it's pointing towards the door!*

T.   *Yes, and away from the Sun. If we were to measure the angle of this tilt with a protractor, we would find that it was 23.5 degrees. I want you to observe the top end of the axis ... this is really important; can you see its direction in relation to the sun?*

As the teacher moved the Earth in its orbit, anticlockwise around the Sun, the children indicated with their fingers that the direction of the tilt was: 'away from the sun' (winter in northern hemisphere) and 'towards the sun' (summer in the northern hemisphere) and 'sort of in the middle' (autumn and spring in the northern hemisphere)

T.   *When the tilt points towards the Sun, we in the northern hemisphere have summer – long days and short nights. This is the midsummer position. What can you tell me about the parts of the Earth that are lit up and those which are in shadow?*

Robert.   *Well there's a lot more light in the northern hemisphere than shadow.*

T.   *Right. And the opposite is the case when the Earth is in the midwinter position (demonstrates). You can see that the reason for this difference in season is all because of the tilt of the Earth's axis.*

*Case 7.* Ref: National Curriculum Attainment Target 1 Strand (iii) Level 3 – 'recognise that their conclusions may not be valid'; and Level 4 – 'draw conclusions which link patterns in observations'; Strand (i) Level 3 – 'suggest questions and predictions based on everyday experience which can be tested'.

A teacher of a class of 10 to 11 year olds encouraged his children to look for science topics and graphical information in newspapers, on a regular basis, and pin them on a notice board. He extended the activity by looking at advertising and general articles critically, and used a

*Figure 2.4* Explaining midsummer in the northern hemisphere

newspaper with a difference, as a model (see Figure 2.5). *It's not Fair* was the title of a BBC radio programme for schools, broadcast in 1985 under the general title, 'Science Games'. In the programme use was made of *The Daily Fib*, to highlight in a jovial way, certain features of irresponsible journalistic writing.

 ACTIVITY 2.3  CREATE A NEWSPAPER

1.  How many 'not fair' statements can you detect in Figure 2.5? Make a list before reading any further. (Then refer to Appendix I.)
2.  If possible create a class newspaper which illustrates that your pupils are aware:

    - that articles in newspapers can be misleading without being untrue;
    - advertising claims are frequently 'not fair' – statistics can be manipulated;

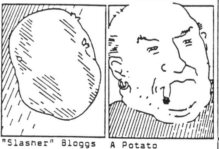

*Figure 2.5*  The Daily Fib

- 'evidence' should be weighed carefully and looked at with a healthy scepticism.

3.  Alternatively, or in addition, find controversial issues in more than one newspaper which force one to weigh the evidence presented. Who are the 'experts', and upon what evidence can we make decisions? Which 'knowers' can we trust? Also, find examples of misleading statements from current newspapers.

## HOW CONTENT IS REPRESENTED IN TEXTBOOKS

Simply *knowing* that the use of appropriate representations in teaching will help pupils learn more effectively, is not enough. There is a need to find a source of good ideas, to complement those which teachers create for themselves. In general, teachers refer to textbooks or journals such as *Primary Science Review*. Although textbooks provide a reservoir of conceptual ideas, pictorial and graphical representations for teaching, the value of these images for teachers with little science background has been questioned.

One American study, albeit at secondary level, has important messages for primary teaching too. Whereas more knowledgeable teachers were confident enough to reorganise a text, and add their own ideas, those teachers with less knowledge followed the text more closely and deleted sections that they did not understand; they maintained their own errors about the content, even when the text contradicted them! It is clear that without understanding science concepts, teachers are unable to diagnose the accuracy or adequacy of the content knowledge presented in textbooks for planning.

As we have pointed out before there isn't one 'right' form of representation. Your choice will in part be governed by how acquainted you are with the subject matter and the language that is being used. Activity 2.4 will help you to make decisions about how to select representations in texts. See also Figure 2.6 (a–e).

ACTIVITY 2.4  JUDGING REPRESENTATIONS

1.  Look carefully at the sample of text illustrations in Figure 2.6 (a–e) and the notes on each below. How appropriate are they for the class you are teaching? In making your judgement, consider:

- the science facts or concepts involved;
- the age and abilities of your pupils;
- how they learn and the language they are capable of using.

Are the representations suitable for them? If not, how would you modify them?

2.  Consider the textbooks *you* use to acquire science information. Select a number of pictorial representations and analogies. Judge them critically. Can you improve on the authors' representations to suit your needs?

LIVERPOOL JOHN MOORES UNIVERSITY
LEARNING SERVICES

**How does one go about learning to use instructional representations?**

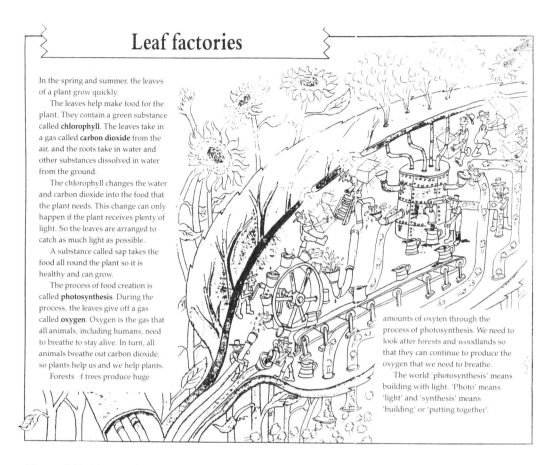

## Leaf factories

In the spring and summer, the leaves of a plant grow quickly.

The leaves help make food for the plant. They contain a green substance called **chlorophyll**. The leaves take in a gas called **carbon dioxide** from the air, and the roots take in water and other substances dissolved in water from the ground.

The chlorophyll changes the water and carbon dioxide into the food that the plant needs. This change can only happen if the plant receives plenty of light. So the leaves are arranged to catch as much light as possible.

A substance called sap takes the food all round the plant so it is healthy and can grow.

The process of food creation is called **photosynthesis**. During the process, the leaves give off a gas called **oxygen**. Oxygen is the gas that all animals, including humans, need to breathe to stay alive. In turn, all animals breathe out carbon dioxide, so plants help us and we help plants.

Forests  f trees produce huge amounts of oxyten through the process of photosynthesis. We need to look after forests and woodlands so that they can continue to produce the oxygen that we need to breathe.

The world 'photosynthesis' means building with light. 'Photo' means 'light' and 'synthesis' means 'building' or 'putting together'.

*Figure 2.6(a)* Instructional representation taken from MacLeod, S., Skelton, M. and Stringer, J. (1989) *Flowering Plants*, Aylesbury: Ginn, p. 8

The explanation is meant to be simple, at a level of 'it's just like . . .' i.e. photosynthesis is just like a factory; miniature men inside the leaf are catching sunlight in boxes, supplying the machine with water, filling cans with a product and sending it down the stem tube. Try to relate, as a child might, the process of photosynthesis, the liberation of oxygen and the factory excess water, with what you know of the biochemical process. What other visual material would you use to complement this analogy?

Cut out two pieces of paper so that they look like inclined planes, one shallow and one steep.
Wrap each piece of paper round a pencil and you will see that each one forms a screw.

Which inclined plane (A or B) would need less effort?
Which screw (a or b) would need less effort?

A screw is used to exert a large force in a nut and bolt, a vice and a car-jack.

*Figure 2.6(b)* Instructional representation taken from Johnson, K. (1991) *Physics for You*, Cheltenham: Stanley Thornes, p. 126

Children have difficulty explaining what a machine is. We often use a machine to increase the force we can exert with our muscles; machines such as levers, gears, pulleys, slopes and screws, enable us to move or do something more easily. When a heavy trolley is pushed up a shallow ramp, the force used over this relatively long distance is much less than the force needed to lift the load straight upwards. Builders use a slope of planks attached to scaffolding to move materials into a house, rather than lift materials to the first floor. The thread of the screw is really a slope wrapped around the screw as the diagram shows.

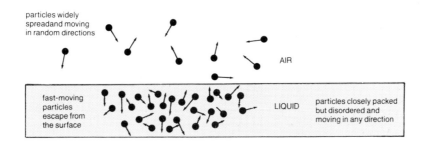

*Figure 2.6(c)* Instructional representation taken from Levinson, R. (1991) *Investigating Materials: Inside Story*, Bath Science 5–16, Walton-on-Thames: Nelson, p. 34

In the context of investigating materials, this illustration represents the way faster moving particles of a liquid escape from the surface of a liquid. In the preceding text, photographs of people were used: as models of a solid (soldiers on parade), a liquid (a crowded street scene) and a gas (people, widely spaced, moving around a corner). How might you develop the diagram to explain the change of state from the liquid to solid using both images? Would you mention energy changes?

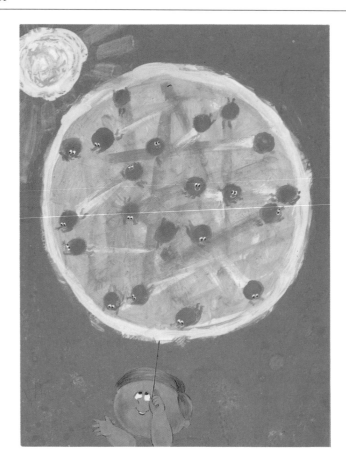

*Figure 2.6(d)* Instructional representation taken from Wilson, N. and Smith, R. (1970) *If I Were an Atom*, Victoria, Australia: Hutchinson.

This painting attempts to explain the behaviour of the invisible world of atoms to young children. The accompanying text says,

    If I were an atom in a balloon, which was heated by the sun,
I would move faster, and so would all the other atoms.
And we would hit the inside of the balloon harder, and more often, and the balloon would get bigger.

Would you consider using humanoid atoms to explain the nature of processes such as melting, dissolving, evaporation and condensation? Is it appropriate to humanise particles to introduce children to the kinetic theory?

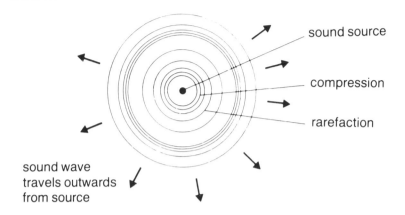

sound source

compression

rarefaction

sound wave
travels outwards
from source

*Figure 2.6(e)* Instructional representation taken from Bradley, L., Green, H., Hoare, J., Jeffery, L. and Witton, N. (1992) *Discovering Connections: Sounding Off (Key Stage 1 Teachers' Resource Pack)* Bath Science 5–16, Walton-on-Thames, Nelson, p. 34

The associated text to this diagram mentions that sound waves are caused by vibrating objects and that the air is alternately compressed and rarefied. How might you use this diagram with a slinky spring to make the understanding of this concept easier?

There are other ways of learning to translate content knowledge for learners than modifying ideas from texts. Newly qualified teachers have to learn on the job, trying things out and learning from others; listening to experienced teachers tell stories of what worked for them is important. Research indicates that the stories experienced teachers tell are powerful ways of organising knowledge, of 'best' examples, explanations that 'work' and curriculum know-how. However good the story, it may need modification, for teaching is about making *personal* meaning. When you understand, your task is then to create a form that your pupils will also understand; it's personal for them too.

## SUMMARY

One of the most important elements of the science knowledge base is that which deals with a subject's teachability, making it comprehensible to others. Understanding subject knowledge helps teachers explain more effectively; they are able to translate it in different ways to suit different groups of learners. There is never one 'right' form of representation.

Instructional representations can take many forms. They can be verbal and/or non-verbal, for example, drawings, graphics and models. It is important that their purpose is made clear to the class. Representations can be judged in terms of their usefulness, appropriateness and correctness; these criteria can be applied to those in textbooks or those that are homemade. Personal understanding of subject content is vital to make these judgements.

# Unit 3

# Restructuring children's understanding

## 'I'VE NEVER UNDERSTOOD THAT UNTIL NOW!'

These were the words of a teacher, during an in-service course, who suddenly had understood an abstract idea. He realised that the electrons within an electric circuit were not supplied solely by the battery, but were part of the material of the wires. Understanding had been helped by the course organiser using cross-sectional diagrams of a battery, bulb and the wires. After discussion and explanation, the teacher was able to realise the specific purposes of the materials involved, as well as gaining a more complete understanding of how a simple circuit works (see Appendix II for this teacher's progression in understanding). To supplement the diagrams the course organiser used an analogy: the movement of electrons in a circuit was like that of beads in a necklace that can be moved around the string. The beads represented the electrons in the wires when they are 'pushed' round by a battery.

These two forms of instructional representation were appropriate for the teacher audience. The course organiser was able to select them appropriately and use them effectively, as a direct result of her subject knowledge of electricity and pedagogical knowledge in that context.

It is unfortunate that the 'Eureka!' experience of the teacher, in realising the origin of the electrons in the electric current, may not be so obviously matched by equivalent revelations for children. At least, the research on conceptual change teaching reports that the task of restructuring children's knowledge is no easy matter. Learners have well established conceptions that may remain different from those of scientists, regardless of the clarity with which teachers put over ideas! It is clear that learning is much more than mere addition of new ideas to a person's knowledge. Yet any change in mental structures may be very difficult to detect, for it involves children in using language which may be inadequate to express their understanding. Intuitive ideas about science may remain unaffected by teaching correct adult versions of science; children may select their teacher's version or keep their own or keep both versions side by side to use in different contexts. This unit outlines the importance of recognising misconceptions or so-called 'alternative frameworks' in children. It then provides an account of the way one teacher helped children to shift their understanding by challenging some of their misconceptions, on a topic of forces and energy.

## MISCONCEPTIONS OR 'ALTERNATIVE FRAMEWORKS'

What's all the fuss about? What's in children's heads that needs to be altered? Children, and adults, have their own ideas about science, and this intuitive knowledge when used to explain central concepts, may be incompatible with the scientific view. Everyone agrees that these 'everyday' ideas are, in general, sensible and plausible. That is, they are based on what, to the individual, is valid reasoning and evidence; but they are not 'correct'. For example, to many children gravity is strongly associated with the presence of air, and increases as the distance above the Earth's surface is increased; the eye is thought to produce the light by which we see; humans are not thought of as animals; and forces are often thought of as being something inside a moving body, acting in the direction of motion, (e.g. 'the force of a hit on a golf-ball was still on it for a while and gradually wore off!'). Some attempts have been made to quantify the prevalence of these 'alternative frameworks'. Watts (1983), for example, describes eight distinctive frameworks that pupils use when describing events involving the concept of force. Researchers have indicated that at all levels, from children of school age to graduates, and across different science content areas, personal understandings frequently run contrary to consensus scientific views. These misconceptions, 'alternative conceptions' or 'alternative frameworks' are well documented in the literature, (e.g. Driver, 1983; Osborne, 1985; Driver *et al.*, 1985).

While there has been concern about the desirability of introducing scientific concepts to children at too young an age, the consequence of not doing so may well mean that older children form inaccurate and/or inflexible frameworks that make further learning increasingly difficult (see the example in Appendix II). The alternative framework can be a straitjacket on thinking. Therefore it is crucial to be aware of misconceptions of children in the classroom, and to provide appropriate instructional representations to move their thinking forward, along scientific lines. A curriculum development which has capitalised on recognising these alternative frameworks is the Nuffield Primary Science series (1993).

 ## ACTIVITY 3.1  DEALING WITH SOME MISCONCEPTIONS OF CHILDREN

Finding out about children's alternative frameworks is only the first step in helping them change their beliefs. The second step is to take a deliberate move to help them replace non-scientific, conflicting ideas with acceptable scientific ones. Consider how you might offer children a scientific view for the following misconceptions:

1.  'A worm is an insect' (age 8).
2.  'All rocks are grey and hard' (age 7).
3.  'Snow is made from frozen rain' (age 8).

4.    'Metals stick to magnets like glue' (age 9).

Think carefully about the nature of the task you will offer:

How do you intend to involve children in reflecting on their existing beliefs?
Will your instructional representation take the form of more talk with the children, an explanation by you or practical investigations?
Do you intend to work in groups, to allow the children to discuss evidence for their own everyday ideas?
Does the task allow for genuine group cooperation? (see examples in Dunne and Bennett, 1990).

---

The implication from many research findings is that teachers should explicitly plan to restructure children's knowledge. Basically, conceptual change teaching involves helping children to articulate openly what they think and to challenge their own misconceptions by using a variety of teaching strategies. The methods which teachers select depend as much on their children's levels of understanding, as on their own pedagogical and subject content knowledge.

## A THEORETICAL MODEL OF OPERATION

Cosgrove and Osborne (1985) offer a model of conceptual change, 'The Generative Learning Model' (Figure 3.1) which describes in theory the activities in which the teacher and children are involved. The authors describe the need for 'preconditions' to this model:

1.    Teachers need to identify the children's personal views about the science they are studying.
2.    The learners need to explore the concepts in everyday situations and examine their own views.
3.    A class environment needs to be a non-threatening one, in which children's views can be exposed without fear of ridicule.

These preconditions, therefore, have a direct influence on the teaching strategies employed.
    The term generative (i.e. generating meaning) is synonymous with constructive (i.e. constructing meaning) and is based on the ideas of Wittrock (1974) where teachers must:

> find the meanings and concepts that the learner has generated already from his or her background, attitudes, abilities and experiences and  determine ways so that the learner will generate new meanings and concepts that will be useful to him or her.

The model has been selected because it identifies the separate 'activities' the teacher and pupil perform in conceptual change teaching.

| Phase | Teacher Activity | Pupil Activity |
|---|---|---|
| **Preliminary** | Ascertains pupils' views; classifies these; seeks scientific views; identifies historical views; considers evidence which led to abandoning old views. | Completes surveys, or other activities, designed to pin-point existing ideas. |
| **Focus** | Establishes a context. Provides motivating experiences. | Becomes familiar with the materials used to explore the concept. |
| | Joins in, asks open-ended personally-orientated questions. | Thinks about what is happening, asks questions related to the concept. |
| | Interprets pupil responses. | Decides and describes what he/she knows about the events, using class and home inputs. |
| | | Clarifies own view on the concept. |
| | Interprets and elucidates pupils' views. | Presents own view to (a) group (b) class, through discussion and display. |
| **Challenge** | Facilitates exchange of views. Ensures all views are considered. Keeps discussion open. | Considers the view of (a) another pupil (b) all other pupils in class, seeking merits and defects. |
| | Suggests demonstrative procedures, if necessary. | Tests the validity of views by seeking evidence. |
| | Presents the evidence for the scientists' view. | Compares the scientists' view with class's view. |
| | Accepts the tentative nature of pupils' reaction to the new view. | |
| **Application** | Contrives problems which are most simply and elegantly solved using the accepted scientific view. | |
| | Assists pupils to clarify the new view, asking that it be used in describing all solutions. | Solves practical problems using the concept as a basis. |
| | Ensures students can verbally describe solutions to problems. | Presents solutions to others in class. |
| | Teacher joins in, stimulates, and contributes to discussion on solutions. | Discusses and debates the merits of solutions; critically evaluates these solutions. |
| | Helps in solving advanced problems; suggests places where help might be sought. | Suggests further problems arising from the solutions presented. |

*Figure 3.1*  The 'Generative Learning Model' of Cosgrove and Osborne

**The model in action: a case study of teaching forces and energy**

We have here used the model (Figure 3.1) to analyse a case study, showing how its components work in practice. A class of 9–11 year olds was investigating forces and energy in the context of 'moving toys'. In planning the teacher used the Programme of Study for Attainment Target 4, Physical Processes, Strands (ii) and (iii).

More precisely the experiences within the classroom were designed to develop their understanding of forces and their effects, and energy transfer, through activities using a number of toy cars. The teacher firmly believed that the class's procedural knowledge would work alongside and strengthen the children's content knowledge, about forces and energy. She was influenced by Lawson (1991):

acquisition of declarative (content) knowledge is very much a constructive process that makes either implicit or explicit use of procedural knowledge.
 To teach science effectively teachers need to know how to help students participate in the constructive process, because doing so improves meaningfulness and retention of the declarative knowledge and increases consciousness and generizability of the procedural knowledge (our brackets).

It is this pupil participation that the teacher aimed for, and her sequence of lessons is described using the model's headings.

**Preliminary phase**

The sessions began with the teacher asking questions about how a toy car she had placed on the table could be moved. The children offered ideas such as 'push it', 'blow it', 'pull it', 'with string' and 'put it on a slope'. These ideas, and others, were accepted and demonstrated by the teacher; then their ideas were written on a large sheet of paper. What they had offered were sorted into 'pushes' and 'pulls'. Putting the idea of a slope under the heading 'pull' led the children to question the teacher's motives.

|  |  |
| --- | --- |
| T. | *Why have I put slope under 'pull'?* |
| Abigail. | *Because the car is pulled down.* |
| T. | *Do I pull it down?* |
| Abigail. | *No, that's string.* |
| T. | *Do we know what pulls the car down?* |
| Darren. | *Gravity.* |
| T. | *That's right. OK. What's gravity?* |
| Phillippa. | *Everything gets pulled to the ground.* |
| Daniel. | *It's a force.* |
| Steven. | *It's an apple.* |
| T. | *Thank you. Everything is pulled to the ground by gravity and gravity is a force. And I have a pretty good idea where the apple story has come from!* |

By asking the children about how the toy car moved, and helping them to organise their ideas into scientifically accepted descriptions of forces (the teacher described a force as a push or a pull) the children were able to challenge and discuss their personal beliefs. The discussion about gravity enabled the teacher to dispel the idea that an apple was a force, by telling a quick story about Sir Isaac Newton. This teaching strategy was chosen because it introduced the specialist vocabulary she wished the children to use, as well as helping to elicit their ideas.

We can see from the preconditions and the preliminary phase of the 'generative' model that these conditions were achieved. The enthusiasm of the class was evident, especially when their group activity was described. From a large collection of toy cars, that moved by a variety of means (e.g. elastic-powered, pull-backs, wind-ups and battery-operated) the class was asked to work in groups of four (their choice) to answer the question, 'How does your toy car move?'

**Focus phase**

By providing the context of moving toy cars as a way of exploring forces, the class was encouraged to discuss the investigations in terms of pulls and pushes. The groups were free to investigate the movement in the way they chose, while the teacher moved around each group and joined in their activities. This gave the teacher the opportunity to question the children's ideas further and develop their responses:

| | | |
|---|---|---|
| | T. | *How are you making your car move?* |
| | James. | *I pull the car back and it winds up inside and goes along.* |
| | T. | *What do you think is inside the car that makes it wind up?* |
| | Carly. | *It's like a spring. A spring in a clock.* |
| | T. | *Do you mean that by pulling the car backwards on the table you are winding up a spring inside?* |
| | Carly. | *When I let go the spring lets go.* |

The form of questioning the teacher used attempted to elicit the child's ideas from direct observation of the car moving, as well as giving practice in using specialist vocabulary in context. The teacher felt confident that the children could make the links between forces and energy (i.e. the spring letting go to push the car along) during the activity; and that this example could then be used as an effective point for discussion later when these links needed to be made more explicit.

An important feature of this session was the class coming together at the end, to talk about their investigations of pushes and pulls, in the light of the original classification on the large sheet of paper. Each group was given time to demonstrate their findings about each car movement, and present these under the headings of 'push' and 'pull'. Many problems arose from this, as the children tried to classify their cars using these terms.

| | | |
|---|---|---|
| | T. | *Where will you put the battery operated car?* |
| | Sarah. | *Well, we don't know if the battery pushes or pulls but we pushed the switch.* (The car went into the 'push' column). |

> T.  *Yes, I can see your problem. I think you have come up with a good explanation but do we need to say more?*
>
> Rachel.  *There's an engine-thing (motor) in my car. You can see it if you take the top off.*
>
> T.  *Does the battery make that motor go round when you switch it on?*
>
> Rachel.  *If you turn the battery round it goes backwards. Look.*
>
> T.  *OK. Let's think about this. Sarah has put the battery-operated car under push because she pushed the switch on to make it work. Rachel has shown us how electricity makes the motor go round; forwards and backwards! Does this help us at all?*
>
> Debbie.  *I think the electricity pushes the motor round which pushes the wheels round and makes the car move.*

A dilemma exists. How much further should such a discussion be taken? Many factors, including time and the ability of the children influence such decisions. In this case the final explanation was felt to be enough and certainly more full than Sarah's explanation about the switch; a significant point here would be whether Sarah had actually 'accepted' this alternative explanation. Again, this was an important issue that the teacher would return to when the class's study developed their ideas on 'energy'; a feature of this work would be on electrical energy. However, in Sarah's defence, to explain the switch as a push is an obvious answer. It's this action she can see.

The investigations and the individual, group and class discussions helped to focus the children's ideas. The teacher's role in eliciting and interpreting these ideas was seen as crucial to the development of the area of study. This ability to allow children to express and challenge their own thinking is fundamental in conceptual change teaching; the generative model of Cosgrove and Osborne provides one way of making this happen. The teacher felt in this case study that her questioning had to be very specific, to challenge and build on what the children had already expressed, and to promote a way of thinking and working.

Jelly (1985) suggests that it is the teacher's questioning that promotes scientific investigation rather than the child's, 'a child's curiosity often does not show itself as spontaneous questioning but rather as a statement of interests'. For example, looking at living things is exciting; an eager child looking at woodlice exclaims, 'They like the stones' and the practised teacher can convert the observation into, 'Do they go where it is damp or where it is dry? Do they go where it is dark or light?' or 'Do they stop moving when they touch something else?' – questions to be followed by, 'How can we check this out?'. As a consequence of this translation the teacher's questioning provides an enquiring environment and opportunities for investigation are not lost.

Jelly provides a most useful list of questions which she labels 'productive' because they stimulate productive activity and 'unproductive', those which do not lead to scientific investigation. She argues that it is the former which need to be encouraged to help children with starting points for scientific enquiry. Productive questions include those that 'promote science as a way of working' and that 'successful answering is achievable by all children'. On the other hand, unproductive questions include those that 'promote science as information' and 'tend to emphasise answering as the achievement of a correct end product'. The following activity (based on Jelly) will help you to develop an awareness of the questions you ask; those which might help direct children's scientific activity ('productive') and those which might help to elucidate understanding ('unproductive').

ACTIVITY 3.2  PRODUCTIVE AND UNPRODUCTIVE QUESTIONS

Try your hand at creating different sorts of questions, both of a 'productive' (i.e. promote science as a way of working) and 'unproductive' (i.e. promote science as information) nature. Provide examples of both types of question, in a context of your choice. (Examples in the context of forces and energy have been provided in Appendix III, by way of illustration).

1.   When are 'unproductive' questions particularly useful?
2.   Improve your questioning. Leave a tape-recorder running when you are teaching science. Later listen to the type of questions you asked. Did you have a range of question types? How did the children respond?
3.   Improve your children's questioning. Discuss and display the questions they ask.

Throughout the focus phase the teacher used a variety of 'productive' and 'unproductive' questions to develop the class's understanding of forces and energy. The class worked individually, (e.g. tackling their own investigation) and in different-sized groups, (e.g. cooperating on a joint investigation about how cars moved) including whole class activity. The latter is illustrated by the development of a concept map to which everyone contributed. Figure 3.2 shows the class's understanding of the concepts involved in the investigation, and the links the children had made between them.

The concept map identified at this stage the children's understanding of the way the toy cars moved. The dotted lines showed tentative links that needed to be resolved. It is this *balance* of working as individuals and in different group sizes which is such an important teaching strategy; children are then able to represent their understanding of the area of study in a variety of ways – this area will be discussed more fully in Unit 5. This case study continued into the next phase of the generative learning model.

**Challenge phase**

This phase has as an overall aim to allow the children to challenge ideas, not only their own, but also the ideas of others, through seeking evidence. The teacher's role here was again to develop the children's ideas towards those accepted by the scientific community. To begin, the teacher recorded the children's ideas, after several investigations, on a large sheet of paper, in the hope that they could be used to initiate challenges to their thinking. These are some of the statements the children gave her:

● There is more gravity higher up the slope so the car goes faster.
● The car uses up energy so it stops moving along.
● The car has more energy on a slope than on a table.
● The more turns on the key the further the wind-up car goes.
● Friction, like bumps, causes the car to slow down.

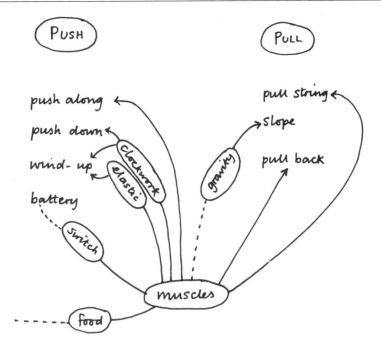

*Figure 3.2* Sorting a collection of toy cars

What seems to have come from this sample of statements is the way the class had identified several explanations for the phenomena they had observed. What is also interesting, but not surprising, is that some of the explanations confuse the concepts of forces and energy, for example, 'there is more gravity higher up the slope so the car goes faster'. Clarifying and challenging these statements was the way the teacher developed this stage. As a way of combining these ideas and describing the concepts of forces and energy, she gathered them together as a whole class. Figure 3.3 shows what she drew. The children's list of statements was kept alongside a large diagrammatic representation of forces and energy, using the idea of a car rolling down a slope.

By representing the concepts of energy and forces in this way, relating directly to their investigations and explanations, many of the children realised that their statements were based on the 'wrong' concept. For example, one child had originally said, 'The car uses up energy so it stops moving along.' The fact that the child described the car slowing down as a result of energy being used up was a clear misconception, as far as energy conservation was concerned. It showed that the child had not fully developed adult ideas about the effects of frictional forces. The dilemma for the teacher is to judge how far to attempt to correct or alter these suggestions. In this case the teacher used the child's 'wrong' concept alongside the explanations about frictional forces used in the diagram; this may have gone some way to dispel this child's misconception.

Read + make notes.

## Accepted Scientific Ideas

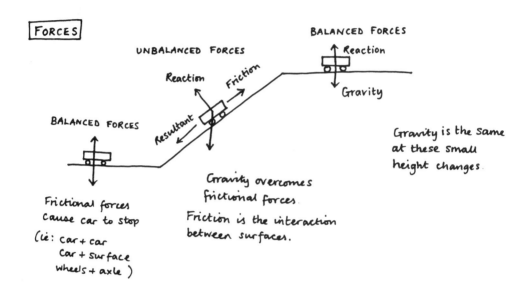

FORCES

UNBALANCED FORCES

BALANCED FORCES

Reaction

Gravity

Reaction    Friction

Resultant

BALANCED FORCES

Gravity is the same at these small height changes.

Frictional forces cause car to stop

(i.e: car + car
Car + surface
wheels + axle )

Gravity overcomes frictional forces.

Friction is the interaction between surfaces.

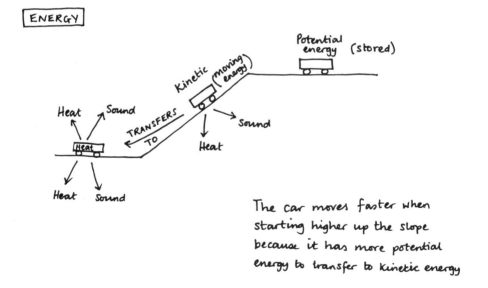

ENERGY

Potential energy (stored)

Kinetic (moving energy)

Heat    Sound

TRANSFERS TO

Sound

Heat

Heat

Heat    Sound

The car moves faster when starting higher up the slope because it has more potential energy to transfer to kinetic energy

The processes of friction cause the transfer of kinetic energy to heat and sound.

Figure 3.3 Instructional representation of forces and energy

## Application phase

To analyse a child's shift in thinking with any degree of certainty is very difficult. It may be demonstrated within the application phase where children are invited to apply their ideas. Towards the end of the term, the children were asked to design and make a toy that moved by a push or a pull. This technology activity required that the children understood the ideas behind the concept of forces, (i.e. pushes and pulls) and energy (i.e. transfer and conservation) and were able to put them into another context (i.e. making their own moving toy). Alongside this manufacturing process, the class's language work was to explain the toy's movements in terms of forces and energy. One particular child in the case study designed a windmill that worked by a mass falling under gravity, causing string to unwind and so turning the sails of the windmill. Her drawings and explanations for the movement in Figure 3.4 reflect her understanding of forces and energy in this particular context.

The child's design and explanation clearly demonstrate an understanding of some of the concepts involved in forces and energy (e.g. gravity as a force and different forms of energy) even though she uses incorrect specialist vocabulary. Her use of, for example, 'weight' for mass, and her possible confusion over energy 'changes', rather than 'transfers to a different form', might call for immediate discussion and may provide starting points for further work. The degree to which correction is made is again a dilemma the teacher faces.

The children's work gathered over the term was displayed around the room, in addition to secondary sources. The latter have not been discussed so far, but the teacher provided a variety of reference books, videos and posters, presenting ideas about forces and energy and their application in everyday contexts. To invite children to refer to and add to these when they felt the need was an important element in the teacher's classroom management.

The case study demonstrates one teacher's approach to selecting different teaching strategies to help children shift their understanding about two basic scientific concepts. It must be emphasised that both concepts are difficult to teach at any level, and there is no agreement about the most appropriate time to introduce the concepts. Whatever strategy is used, at whatever stage, the question must be asked about its effectiveness. How does one get a 'window on the mind' to see what the children have understood? The teacher observed carefully the work individuals had done in investigation, discussion and written work and used a class concept map as one particular tool to assess their corporate understanding, Figure 3.5.

The demands of this way of working are great and require flexibility to shift from one teaching strategy to another; a skill which has recently been highlighted is of great importance, (Alexander *et al.*, 1992). The final activity provides an opportunity to address Alexander's recommendation by planning a sequence of lessons to incorporate a variety of teaching strategies; a balance of 'telling' strategies with 'finding out for self', experimental work with non-experimental activity, working individually and working with others and so on.

Windy Windmill

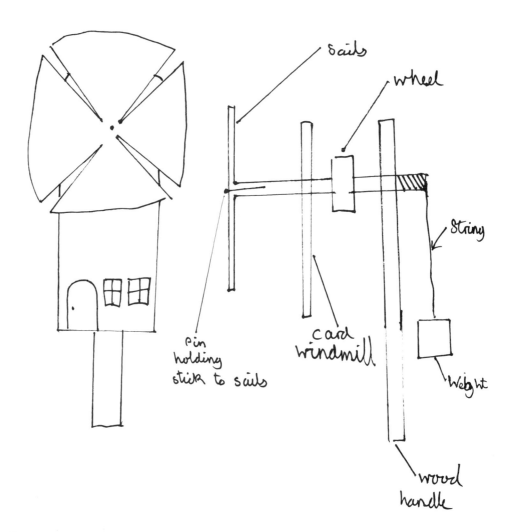

Sails

wheel

Pin
holding
stick to sails

card
windmill

String

Weight

wood
handle

"We put energy into the coil, it drops the weight and turns the stick. Then energy changes into a different form so the coil unturns totally and the sails stop moving."

"Gravity pulls the weight down towards the ground which uncoils the string which turns the stick."

Figure 3.4  A child's design and explanation of her toy's movement

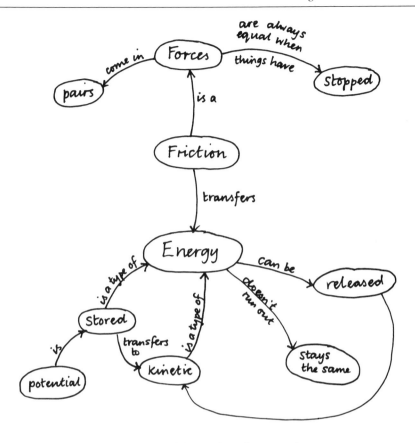

*Figure 3.5* A class concept map at the end of the study on forces and energy

## ACTIVITY 3.3  A BALANCE OF TEACHING STRATEGIES

Part of the recent research in the Leverhulme Primary Project (Bennett and Carré, 1993) was to observe student-teachers and newly qualified teachers teaching science. The following is a list of teaching strategies, and their associated task, that the various teachers used when translating the Programmes of Study into reality:

| *Teaching strategy* | *Task* |
|---|---|
| 1. Read and find information: | Look at two texts to explore how fossils are formed |
| 2. Listen to an explanation: | Listen to an account of the way fertilisation in flowers is achieved |
| 3. Follow written instructions: | Use Technic Lego to study the effect of using different-sized gear wheels |

I.M. MARSH LIBRARY LIVERPOOL L17 6BD
TEL. 0151 231 5216/5299

| 4. | Design and/or make: | (a) Design a sun dial; (b) make a mangonel (a medieval machine for hurling stones in war) |
| 5. | Problem solve: | Make a machine that travels a metre and stops |
| 6. | Prove that: | Verify the magnetic effect of electricity on a compass |
| 7. | Survey: | Collect data on the rocks and living things in and on a wall |
| 8. | Part of an investigation: | Describe a pattern from data |
| 9. | Whole investigation: | How is the fall of a parachute affected by changing the independent variables? |

Plan a series of lessons, in a content area and class of your own choosing. Show how you would use a variety of teaching strategies (those suggested and others) to give a balance to the overall structure of the study. Try to include individual study and work for different-sized groups, including whole class work.

Which strategy best might best promote the understanding of difficult concepts?

How will you empower the children to investigate their own problems in terms of their intuitive knowledge?

## SUMMARY

This unit shows the need for a variety of teaching methods to help children restructure their own understanding. Teachers have to balance the National Curriculum demands (the correctness of adult science as stated in the Statements of Attainment), with getting children to make sense of their worlds in their own terms; at times accepting where they're at, even if it is some place other than the 'right answer'.

The duty of a teacher lies in setting the conditions that are necessary for conceptual change teaching; a means of helping children shift from a 'right answer' belief grounded in plausible personal experience, towards more acceptable adult science 'right answers'. Preconditions to the generative learning model clearly require a teacher's understanding of subject content knowledge, pedagogical knowledge and how children learn.

# Teachers' planning and learners' progression

## DILEMMAS

In general, learners' progression refers to the proposed sequence in their development, of skills and content knowledge, and teachers use this idea to plan meaningful programmes of work. Two major dilemmas exist:

1. Individuals do not necessarily progress along the National Curriculum's suggested pattern; their rate of progress is neither constant nor necessarily linear.
2. Although we have stressed a view of learning which emphasises individual differences, there is still a need for progression along general lines.

Therefore the teacher's concern is to plan for the progression of 30-plus diverse learners, within the generalised requirements of the National Curriculum. This unit looks first at the complexity of teachers' planning and then at the diversity of learners' progression; within this, further dilemmas and unintentional mismatches exist.

## AN EXAMPLE OF MISMATCH

A teacher's initial plan, devised for a study of flowering and non-flowering plants, looked like this (the National Curriculum levels shown for Attainment Target 2 are in brackets):

|     |     |     |
| --- | --- | --- |
| (a) | Survey of school grounds – compare with local pond | (1b & 2c) |
| (b) | Sorting flowering and non-flowering plants, keys | (2b & 4b) |
| (c) | Plant growth: investigating factors; light, water and temperature ... grass/buttercup comparison | (2a & 3c) |
| (d) | Plant reproduction: buttercup | (4a & 5a) |

The teacher described this half-term's plan in more detail by referring to the requirements of the Programmes of Study for Attainment Target 2, Strand (i): 'Pupils should be introduced to the . . . organ systems of flowering plants. They should investigate the factors that effect plant growth, for example, light intensity, temperature and amount of water' and Strand (ii): 'They should have the opportunity to develop skills in identifying locally occurring species of plants by observing structural features and making and using simple keys'.

When looking at the assessment criteria supplied by the Statements of Attainment, it would appear that a clear progression from levels 1 to 5 could be achieved. However, in reality, the level and scope of an individual's progression in understanding may not match this theoretical model offered by the National Curriculum.

Here are two examples that reiterate this last point. They arose from the above planned programme of work on plants. In talking to Lucy and Jemma, both 9 years old, the teacher inferred from Lucy's statements that her understanding of plants was limited to school knowledge. In many ways it reflected the expected sequence, whereas Jemma had had a wider experience of plants and gardening at home. Table 4.1 shows selected statements made by the two girls when questioned by their teacher. The statements relate directly to the teacher's plans, with tentative suggestions for each child's level of understanding.

It is difficult to judge what understanding lies behind what a child says, but this example does indicate the possible mismatch that can exist between the planned sequence of work and children's understanding.

## PROGRESSION THROUGH PLANNING QUESTIONS

Research into the structure of children's concepts by Preece (1978) and others, suggests the necessity for flexibility in ordering the curriculum, and Taylor (1990) has recently raised doubts about the sequence of Statements of Attainment as signposts of progression in the National Curriculum. How can teachers plan with these ideas in mind?

The following programme of work on fossils develops the notion of flexibility in planning

Table 4.1  Lucy's and Jemma's levels of understanding

| Lucy | Jemma |
|------|-------|
| (a)  I've learned that the school grounds have lots of different plants, and so does the pond. (1b) | (a)  I already know that the school grounds have different plants and we've got a pond at home. (1b) |
| (b)  I think I know the difference between plants but the key was very difficult. (2b?) | (b)  I know the difference between plants. I've used a key like that before. (4b) |
| (c)  I know the farmer feeds the fields with fertiliser . . . I think I'm wrong about how plants feed . . . (?) | (c)  At home we have a greenhouse and grow things in special ways. (2a; 3c) |
| (d)  I can draw the buttercup picture very well but I can't really see the bits inside the real buttercup. (?) | (d)  I know about pollen and insects because I've seen this happen in our garden. (4a; 5a ?) |

a topic based on children's interest. Fossils hold a fascination for most children, and the excitement seen when fossils are found or studied is evident. A teacher capitalised on this. The study, over a few weeks, was part of an environmental local study, with a geography bias.

Questions were devised, which were thought to help the children understand the nature of fossils and how they were formed. This approach was felt preferable to the usual topic format, i.e. listing areas of study, because the teacher felt questions could be used more easily to focus a study. Although the questions in the plan, Figure 4.1, were interchangeable in the sequence in which they could be asked, the teacher thought one provided an obvious starting point for her class of 8 to 9 year olds.

A more operational programme of work is given in Table 4.2. (Programmes of Study: Attainment Target Strand 2(ii): 'They should be introduced to how plants and animals can be preserved as fossils.')

What Table 4.2 highlights are the definite points in time for events along the study; for example, the starting point and the organised visit. The flexible nature needed for devising

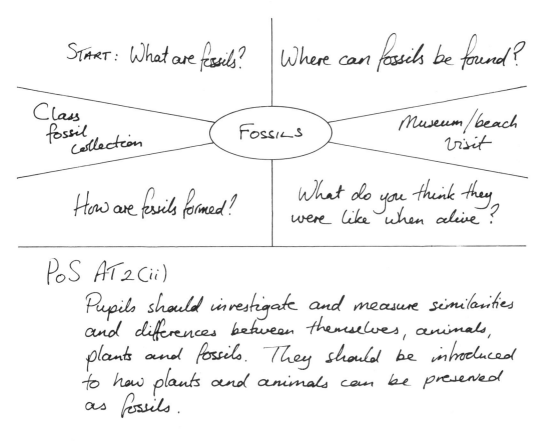

Figure 4.1  A teacher's plan using questions

*Table 4.2* Flexibility in planned activities for a study of fossils

| Starting point | Question | AT 1 | AT 2 |
|---|---|---|---|
| **Fossil collection** | How can we sort our collection? | 1a | Nil |
| | What criteria will we use? | 2a | |
| Fossil samples | Can we build up a picture of what the fossil may have looked like alive? | 1a 2abc | |
| Fossils in rocks | How can we model the burial process involved in formation of fossils? | 2abc 3abcd | |
| **Museum/beach visit** | In which types of rock are the fossils found? | 2abc | |
| | What other information can we find out about their living habits? | | |
| Information from secondary sources | How can we show when our fossils lived? | | |
| | Develop class time-line | | |

the other sessions required the teacher to make choices about:

- capitalising on the previous session's outcomes;
- placing understanding of content and process skills in a variety of different contexts; and
- finding different ways to represent subject content (see Unit 2).

Plans for programmes of work can be looked upon as a proposed pathway of study, which can bend and deviate, but which have definite signposts based on educational and organisational decisions. The questions used to inform the investigations in this example were broad, and became reframed as the programme of work developed.

This example demonstrates progression in terms of the understanding of process skills (procedural progression), as described in Attainment Target 1. However, a further dilemma in planning for progression exists; Attainment Target 2 (conceptual progression) has no mention of fossil work within the Statements of Attainment. The teacher justified her decision to include this work as the locality was a rich source of fossils and local children were aware of their existence. She justified this a stage further as she described conceptual progression in terms of the scientific vocabulary the children would be using; this involved the specialist words associated with fossils, burial and preservation processes.

## PROGRESSION THROUGH PLANNING SPECIALIST VOCABULARY

As an influence in her final decision the teacher was interested in the way Sutton (1992) represents a child's progression in scientific vocabulary. Figure 4.2 shows such a 'burr notation'. The thicker 'hooks' demonstrate the move to the more scientifically accepted words, developed through teaching sequences over time.

Sutton admits that although the 'burr notation cannot cope with all the subtleties of meaning change, it is nevertheless a useful device to start a discussion of those changes, and we can

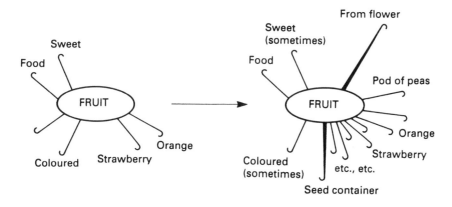

Figure 4.2 The progression in a child's understanding of fruit

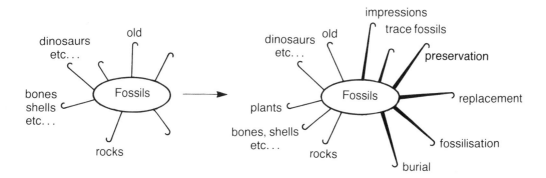

Figure 4.3 Planning for progression in vocabulary in a study of fossils

use it to explore how meanings might change over time'. The teacher did that, as shown in Figure 4.3. She used the burr notation as a means of projecting a possible progression in vocabulary of the class as a whole.

 ACTIVITY 4.1  PLANNING FOR PROGRESSION TO MORE SCIENTIFICALLY
ACCEPTABLE VOCABULARY

Select an area of study. Use the idea of burr notation to project the paths of progression in vocabulary that you may expect, for a particular age group.

So far progression has been described in terms of planning flexible sequences of work; the study of fossils illustrates a way of using questions for this purpose. Questions are used for each probable investigation, in whichever order, to capitalise on children's interests and to enhance the progression of skills, concepts and scientific vocabulary.

It is interesting to record that one group of teachers took this idea of planning, with specific questions in mind, a stage further. The science coordinator helped the staff make decisions about the type of questions in science that would be useful for planning a topic. Purposeful planning in this way ensured that the variety of categories selected would permeate science programmes of work. An example of the record sheet they devised is in Appendix IV.

## PROGRESSION THROUGH PLANNING ACTIVITIES

On another level planning for progression can be achieved by carefully analysing the activities intended for the class. The type of question used to target the investigation can develop progression in terms of conceptual and/or procedural complexity. One newly qualified teacher used the framework shown in Table 4.3 (which he based on the National Curriculum INSET booklet, 1991) to plan questions for progression in process skills. Here are some sequences from his lessons to illustrate how he operated.

His lesson was part of an integrated theme on 'Transport'. It was quite normal for the whole class (9 to 10 year olds) to have an 'in-put' session, to set the scene for the next set of activities, and this was one. The task was presented dramatically, he stood on a table, and the children were totally absorbed in his demonstration:

T.    *We're thinking about what it is that makes something stay up in the air while other things fall straight down through it. I can take two identical pieces of paper. One I can screw up like a ball like this, and I'm going to let go of them and we're going to see what happens. What do you think is going to happen? Any ideas?*

P.    *The one that is screwed up will just fall straight down and the other one will fall, just float down.*

T.    *You think so? Anyone think anything else? Right we'll see what happens.*

Notice that he asked for other ideas and did not simply wait for verification of what he thought would happen. He talked about those who tried to jump off towers at the time of Leonardo da Vinci, and then 'simulated' a parachute jump:

T.    *So I've made my very own parachute. I'm not going to strap myself to it and climb to the top of the building and jump off, because I don't think the parachute would be big enough for me . . . you'll have to pretend that this is me, this green blob of plasticine. Can you do that? What do you think is going to happen?*

P.    *It'll go down really slowly because the air is pushing upwards.*

The teacher chats to the class about what they saw, and invites them to time the descent. He purposely alters the height of drop and they discuss a fair-test.

T. *OK then. So I'm at the same height now, more or less. Three, two, one, I didn't say go did I? Three, two, one, go. How long did that take? It took longer. Why? Was it fair? Not really fair was it, because it hit the table and stopped a bit . . . what sort of things do you think could change how long it takes? What might have an effect on the time it takes for this parachute to fall and hit the ground? What sort of things could influence it. Let's see if we can make a list.*

P. *The size of the parachute.*

T. *The size of the parachute. Right. What do you mean by size? Do you mean how thick it is, how long, how wide?*

It was characteristic of him to challenge pupils' answers. Eventually he included in his list of variables: area of the parachute, its diameter, height of drop, length of strings, turbulence, holes in the surface and weight of the 'body'. Each variable was discussed in turn, with information being drawn from the pupils. He organised different groups to investigate different variables:

T. *This week we are going to test each of these different things to see what effect it actually has on the parachute. I want one group to test one thing from our list and then at the end of the week, on Friday afternoon we'll have one of our sessions when we talk about what we find out, and we'll see if we can put all our test results together to come up with the ideal parachute.*

The children chose the variable they wished to investigate, and the presentation finished with a powerful reminder of the necessity to have a fair-test:

T. *So, if I was thinking about what sort of material we use for the parachute, and I was dropping one from this height made of tissue paper and it took maybe five seconds to fall and then I got another one made out of cast iron, and I dropped it from a mile up and it took six seconds, I couldn't really say that a cast iron parachute is better than a tissue paper one, could I? Because it wasn't a fair-test.*

The pupils designed their own investigation, but within the framework the teacher provided. He frequently asked them to justify their approach or challenged their decisions. With the following group he discussed the factor of turbulence:

P. *There must be no wind though.*

T. *There might be a bit.*

P. *Only a tiny bit.*

T. *That could make a difference couldn't it?*

P. *Yes but it's sheltered quite a bit. If we kept the weight, and thought of that, and had the weight heavier when we were outside than in here.*

T. *But then you'd change the weight and that's another thing changing.*

The effectiveness of the questions he asked were essentially those which said, 'What makes you think that?'. The challenge was to develop the children's confidence to handle an

*Table 4.3* Using questions to plan progression in controlling variables

*Topic*: Transport, flight.
*Year*: 9 to 10 year olds.
*Investigation*: To investigate how the fall of a parachute may be affected by changing one of the independent variables.

| Question | Dependent | Independent | Control |
|---|---|---|---|
| What happens when you drop a piece of paper? Ditto, screwed up? What happens when you drop a parachute? | | | turbulence height shape of paper or parachute shape/size |
| Will the height from which the parachute is dropped make it come down faster? | time | height | weight parachute shape/size turbulence |
| Will the weight change how fast the parachute drops? | time | weight | parachute shape/size height turbulence |
| Will the time taken to fall depend on the size of the parachute or its weight? | time | weight parachute | turbulence height |

(*Note*: The dependent variable is the 'thing' that's being measured, i.e. the outcome, the independent variables are the 'things' that are being tested and the control variables are those that stay the same. See Unit 1.)

increasing complexity of variables. Compare his planned questions in Table 4.3, which shows the overall progression he was aiming for, with what he actually did in class.

Table 4.3 shows the sequence of questions, within the context of parachutes, to help children's understanding of process skills, in particular the increase in complexity of handling variables. Whether a teacher decides to ask a question for assessing children's learning outcomes (e.g. Do you know the variables we need to control in this investigation?) or uses a particular question to differentiate the tasks for particular groups of children (e.g. The progression of difficulty in the parachute questions) depends to a large extent on the teacher's knowledge of the learners. Programmes of work and activities in the classroom need to be flexible in nature and selected for suitable purposes to maximise the progression in children's understanding. Planning thus incorporates long-term and short-term aims, and a justification for the inclusion of areas of study. However, to further complicate the picture, Claxton (1991) makes an important point that no matter how careful the planning, children may see a different picture.

Despite the fact that teachers feel that lessons within a block of work form a well-planned and logical progression, this overview and sense of coherence and cumulativeness is often absent from the student's perception.

Children are likely to be concerned with the immediacy of the moment. For example, when asked to describe what activity they are engaged in, say, within the programme of work on flowering plants, they may happily tell you that they're drawing a flower, sorting seeds or putting a plant in the dark. They tend not to see overall relationships; it is the skill of the teacher to choose suitable teaching strategies and flexible planning that anticipates such incidences, and encourages children to gain a wider perspective.

## A MODEL OF PROGRESSION

Qualter and her colleagues (1990) have advocated a model for progression based on a spiral of science experiences, encompassing the demands of the whole National Curriculum at each Key Stage. The definition for progression given by the authors is 'the expected routes pupils take during the development of their skills, knowledge and understanding'.

The inclusion of the word 'expected' is important as, we have already stated, children progress in different ways. The authors further describe the model as a map that 'does not tell us where to go, but it helps us decide which might be the better routes and how to find where we are'. The model is shown in Figure 4.4.

The model demonstrates the close relationship with the expected conceptual and procedural understanding of children, revisiting these areas of knowledge throughout the Key Stages. Qualter *et al.* describe the model as a conceptual tool to develop learning and assessment activities and each activity (the 'spider' on the model) locates itself between the double pathway, with attachments (the 'legs') representing the understanding of procedures and concepts that would be needed if the activity was to be successfully tackled. The symbols $c, c', c''$, $c'''$ and $p, p', p'', p'''$ represent increasingly difficult concepts and procedures.

In reality however, with an informed knowledge of the learners, this model of progression is not quite so obvious. The model helps us to see a child's possible progression, but it implies a match between levels of conceptual and procedural understanding. As previously stated a correspondence may not be evident; one teacher described an 8 year old child in her class with a hobby in electronics, whose understanding was at least level 5, whereas his procedural understanding was probably hovering around level 2 for Attainment Target 1. Teachers aware of such a mismatch can devise tasks that cater for a combination of levels. The model may be seen better as a rope made up many different threads, and the 'spiders' more like 'millipedes' along the way!

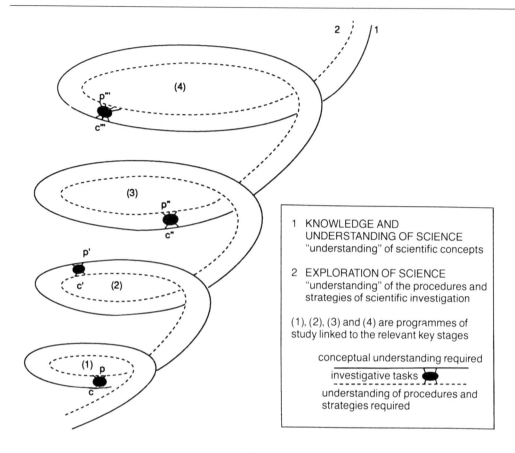

*Figure 4.4* A model of progression

 **ACTIVITY 4.2  DEVISING ACTIVITIES THAT COMBINE DIFFERENT LEVELS OF CONCEPTUAL AND PROCEDURAL KNOWLEDGE**

Statements from 'Materials and their properties' (Attainment Target 3) and Attainment Target 1 Strand (ii) are given below.

Devise a series of questions for investigation that combine across the levels.

*Note*: The links can be matched across, or step up or down the levels to produce a variety of tasks, e.g. 3:2a match with 1:3b – 'Do all "gritty" type rocks make the same amount of sand when rubbed together?'

| *Conceptual knowledge* | *Procedural knowledge* |
|---|---|
| 3:1a  be able to describe the simple properties of familiar materials | 1:1a  observe familiar materials and events |

3:2a  be able to group materials according to observable features

3:3c  understand some of the effects of weathering on buildings and rocks

3:4e  know that weathering, erosion and transport lead to the formation of sediments and different types of soil

3:6h  understand the scientific processes involved in the formation of igneous, sedimentary and metamorphic rocks including the time scales over which these processes operate

1:2b  make a series of related observations

1:3b  observe closely and quantify by measuring using appropriate instruments

1:4b  carry out a fair test ... use appropriate instruments and ... measure quantities

1:5b  choose the range of ... variables to produce meaningful results

1:6b  consider ... range of factors ... identify key variables ... account of qualitative and quantitative observations

What question for investigation would combine 3:2a and 1:1a, or 3:3c and 1:5b?

What other combinations can be successfully demonstrated as questions for activities?

## SMALL SEQUENCES AND INDIVIDUAL PROGRESSION

Whatever form of planning is used, incidental and spontaneous events occur which may not fit the planned schedule! Individuals learn through incidental day to day experiences, and it is the nature of the teacher's responses to a child's question or statement that is vital to encourage these unexpected small step progressions. The following examples show how teachers' responses can enhance a child's learning, redirect it or even negate it.

A class of 7 year olds were on a visit to a park and a child asked, 'Why don't the ducks get their feathers all wet?' The teacher replied, 'Their feathers have a special oil coating them which makes them waterproof ... a bit like the stuff that's coating my wax jacket. It keeps me dry.' The ability of a teacher to answer in such a way, through analogy, is an important issue already discussed in Unit 2. However, on occasions answers cannot be as complete, and a redirection may be more appropriate.

During playtime a 9 year old asked the teacher on duty, 'Why have we got eyebrows?' The teacher said, 'I don't know. Let's go and look it up after play.' On another occasion a 7 year old, investigating floating and sinking said, 'This ball sinks because it is heavy.' The teacher on hearing this said, 'Will all the other balls sink?' The teachers in the last two examples purposely redirected the learning, i.e. by suggesting they together found out about the function of eyebrows or by suggesting an investigation on floating and sinking.

Sometimes however our encounters with children's questions and statements may not encourage learning. A 10 year old was constructing circuits from a worksheet when he asked, 'Why are the bulbs [in parallel] brighter?' The teacher, who may have been feeling uncertain about subject content knowledge, replied, 'We don't need to worry about *why* things are happening, the question asks you *what* is happening. Just answer the question.'

In another example, which related directly to the teacher's planned sequence of work, a 10 year old was sorting rocks by using the rocks' physical properties. The child asked, 'Is this a limestone?' The teacher replied, 'We'll talk about that rock later in another lesson, when we classify them.'

The last two examples illustrate that the actions of teachers reflect their classroom beliefs, i.e. the extended knowledge of parallel circuits was not felt to be relevant, and the rock classification was thought not to be required at that stage of the planned work. It may be said that each child's progression in understanding of circuits and rocks may have been hampered. Yet this is the reality of the classroom. One cannot plan for the perfect progress of each child.

## PERSONAL PATHWAYS OF PROGRESSION

Taking a step back from the classroom and analysing one's own progression in understanding, can make explicit where science ideas were enhanced or where confusion still exists. To recognise one's own level of understanding, one's strengths and weaknesses, is a professional approach to acknowledging the importance of subject matter in teaching. Activity 4.3 invites you to chart your own baseline and progression in a subject area of your choice.

 ### ACTIVITY 4.3  A PERSONAL 'JOURNEY' OF UNDERSTANDING

Select a particular area in science, especially if you have been teaching the subject. Track your progression in understanding to a point of where you are at present. Highlight the important steps in this progression, and acknowledge the outside influences that may have helped or hindered you on the way.

Discuss your present understanding with a trusted friend, to check your degree of understanding. (A real example, developed by a teacher, is given in Appendix II.)

## SUMMARY

Children progress in different ways and this raises many issues in planning for individual learning within general planned programmes of work. A child's development in procedural and conceptual understanding, including progression in scientific vocabulary, can be planned for in the long-term and in the short-term. Teachers have to face a number of dilemmas when planning work for a class of diverse learners; they need to employ different planning strategies to cope with the mismatches that inevitably occur between intended progress and actual outcomes.

# Assessing processes and content

The importance of the variety of forms of assessment and its continuous nature, is emphasised by Mitchell and Koshy (1993):

> Assessing children's learning can take place in a variety of ways across a continuum from very informal, spontaneous, almost 'chance' classroom observations, through to highly structured standardised testing.

Assessment has to be about children's personal achievements, and the variety of methods to expose these achievements must be evaluated frequently. In previous units a number of issues relating to assessment have been raised. Essentially the formative nature of assessment, and the interrelationships between planning, teaching, learning and assessment have been stressed. However, the decisions teachers have to make when assessing any child's achievement and selecting areas for further learning warrants a unit in itself.

Any method a teacher uses in assessing a child's understanding cannot possibly create the whole picture; assessment can be likened to a photograph of a football match – both give a snapshot of an instant in time, which can hardly hope to capture the extra knowledge a child possesses, or the many aspects of the rest of the game. Nevertheless snapshots are useful. They need to be analysed and built upon to come closer to the whole picture; the more varied the forms of assessment, the clearer the picture is likely to be. Assessing what a child says, does and records (writes, draws, models etc.) focuses this challenge, but as every teacher knows these aspects may not occur together. The following examples illustrate this point:

## ASSESSING WHAT CHILDREN SAY AND RECORD

The National Curriculum expects that children should:

AT4:2e    'know that the Earth, Sun and Moon are separate bodies';

AT4:4e   'be able to explain day and night, day length and year length in terms of the movements of the Earth around the Sun'.

It is no easy matter to assess such content. For example, a 9 year old was asked to explain why it gets dark at night. Giles was reluctant to put his ideas on paper, and found writing difficult. He wrote, in Figure 5.1: 'It's dark at night because the moon isn't as bright as the sun, because the Earth turns around.'

Notice how he used the diagram (Figure 5.1) to help him communicate. In the original, both the Sun and the Moon have yellow rays coming from them; yet his teacher knew he understood more than that! Giles was later asked to explain in his own words, on two separate occasions, why night occurs. He said:

Giles.   *The sun shines and it doesn't get to the other half (of the Earth) and only a little is reflective from the moon because of its long journey.*

. . .

Giles.   *Because the Earth is in between the Moon and the Sun and then when the Moon is on one side it's just shining a little so it doesn't light up the whole Earth – half the Earth. So half is light and dark is night, so . . .*

T.   *Where does the light come from?*

Giles.   *The Sun . . . inside the Sun . . . because the lava's so hot it makes it glow very bright.*

*Figure 5.1* A 9 year old's explanation of night and day

What the diagram and the transcripts show is the way teachers have to sift through the evidence that a child may provide to make steps towards some form of assessment. Giles has knowledge about the Sun, Moon and Earth being separate bodies, for the diagram indicates this. Do we infer these bodies are spherical? His statements are a little more problematic – are they at level 4? Would the teacher need to provide another line of questioning, or activity, that would demonstrate a further clarification of his understanding? Being aware of what the child knows, being able to transfer this into an assessable form is one of the many decisions a teacher must make in assessing the child's scientific achievements.

### ACTIVITY 5.1  ASSESSING A CHILD'S RECORDING OF A TIME-LINE

A teacher and her class of 7 year olds spent a series of sessions studying a fossil collection. She then set the following task:

How can we show when fossil animals and plants were alive, and when they became extinct?

The groups researched, using secondary sources, the approximate time scales that their collection of fossils depicted, then placed them on a large class time-line. Alison, aged 7, wrote this account of the task, as shown in Figure 5.2:

How would you assess Alison's understanding from her piece of work? What does her record tell us about her understanding of:

1.  the nature of the task?
2.  her knowledge of time-lines?
3.  her use of scientific vocabulary?

*Figure 5.2* Alison's time-line description

Alison showed immense interest in the task, and wanted to compare the distribution of different types of the same kind of fossil (ammonite) on the time-line. The secondary resources were inadequate for this scrutiny. When she was asked why she wanted to do this, she said that she knew that the ammonites changed a lot over time because she had had this described to her on a recent museum visit. How does this new insight help assess Alison's understanding?

What children say and record give us insight into their conceptual and procedural understanding. When they are eager to communicate they do so with a certain intent, to inform, persuade or whatever. However, what they say or record may provide a distorted reflection of what they 'know'; as seen in the above examples. However good the communication, the listener has to *infer meaning*; no one ever knows exactly what another person means, because each of us has ideas which have arisen from one's unique mental 'picture' of the world, constructed from personal experiences. Hence the unfairness of too hasty assessment of one piece of work!

Examples of children's work are provided in Activity 5.2. The selection has been chosen to illustrate the way writing and diagrammatic recording methods are used by children in a *knowledge-transforming* process, rather than mere copying or regurgitation by rote. The National Writing Project (National Curriculum Council) has produced many excellent books to illustrate the various ways that children are able to write to represent content, with different purposes and audiences in mind (e.g. *Writing and Learning, Becoming a Writer, Audiences for Writing*, published in 1990, Walton-on-Thames: Nelson). There is also a book on the assessment of writing. What is evident from the children's work is that writing performance is strongly related to the nature of the task; better where the child has some control over what is written and the purpose is clear. Children find it easier to write when they have something to write about and the immediacy of science involvement provides just that, often in dramatic ways.

 **ACTIVITY 5.2  LOOKING CLOSELY AT CHILDREN COMMUNICATING**

1.  Examine Figures 5.3–5.8 with the notes provided on each.
2.  Note how the teachers intervened in the writing process, i.e. made clear the purpose for writing.
3.  Judge whether you think the task helped the children make sense of the science in which they were engaged. The focus is on interpretation and flexible use of science knowledge.
4.  Was the task sufficiently interpretative to help diagnose error or partial understanding? Remember that you are assessing the writing and not the writer! Does the writing enable you to judge which part of the National Curriculum is 'understood'? How might you respond to the writer?

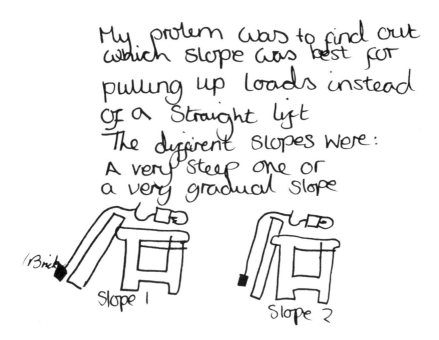

My prolem was to find out which slope was best for pulling up loads instead of a Straight lift
The different slopes were:
A very steep one or a very gradual slope

Slope 1

Slope 2

*Figure 5.3* An example of 'small step' writing in science

There is a place for writing up whole investigations, along the lines of 'what we did', 'what we expected to find' and 'what we found out'. However, writing up 'whole' science reports after an investigation is often a slow and difficult task for many children. Opportunities exist for writing before and during science investigations; 'small step' writing tasks result in less writing overall, frequent and brief, rather than occasional and lengthy. Figure 5.3 is an example of a 'small step' writing task, given before the investigation. This 10 year old was asked to restate her problem, in her own words, to help her focus on what she was about to do. (Other ideas for writing tasks with specific purposes are included in Appendix V.)

Having read the story of *The Paper Bag Princess* (Munsch, R., 1982, London: Scholastic), a class of 9 year olds discussed many aspects of this delightful story, not least the role of the heroine in the story and her character. One child suggested that the Princess had very good hearing and that's why she could hear dragons from afar. Were not all girls better at hearing than boys? Julie-Ann's writing task was focused on the list of variables to keep constant, emphasising the fair-test, before the investigation started. It was another 'small step' type of writing; notice how the amount of writing in the 'method' and 'result' sections is reduced. Points 5 and 8 need explanation: the children were concerned that to be fair everyone had to be healthy, a cold would impair hearing; 'stand back to front' insists that the pupil being tested should not face the pupil dropping the pin. How might the teacher have helped them answer the investigation question? See Figure 5.4 overleaf.

# How good is our Hearing?
## What is a fair test?

1 Make Sure there are no noises. (Silence)
2 Use the Same pin
3 Use the Same Suface
4 Drop from the Same hieght.
5 health of people has to be the Same
6 The Same distance
7 Same pin
8 Always Stand back to front.

| | Stuart | Andrew | Redica | Me |
|---|---|---|---|---|
| 1 mtr | ✓ | ✓ | ✓ | ✓ |
| 2 mtr | ✓ | ✓ | ✓ | ✓ |
| 3 mtr | ✓ | ✓ | ✓ | ✓ |
| 4 mtr | ✓ | ✓ | ✓ | ✓ |
| 5 mtr | ✓ | ✓ | ✓ | ✓ |

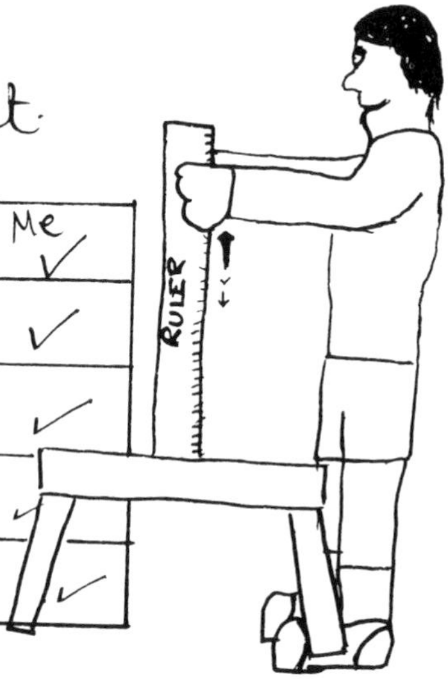

## What we did.

First we got a 30 cm ruler and a Meter-Stick and a pin We then mesured I meter and listened We all heard it. We did the same With 2mtr's 3mtrs 4mtrs and 5mtr's

Julie-Ann.

Figure 5.4 Do girls hear better than boys?

A class of 7 year olds was studying 'sound', a mix of music and science sessions. The children had made beaters, shakers and rattles and had blown down tubes of various shapes and sizes. They had felt the vibrations of a loudspeaker, and seen puffed cereal bounce on top of a drum when tapped. They had plucked rubber bands and investigated the differences their thickness and length made to the sound. The children became involved in percussion too, and one group realised that they could send sounds to the next classroom by tapping on the central heating pipes. The investigation of sound travelling through wooden rulers followed. The word 'vibrations' was commonly used in discussing the cause of sound. See Figure 5.5.

1 We used a stopwatch and a metre rule to work with to try to find out how sound waves travel.

2 We put the metre ruler in Jonathans ear and he could hear the stopwatch which was held on the other end of the ruler.

3. Christopher found out that if you put your ear against the three rulers you could hear the vibrations travelling up to Jonathans ear. me all listened with our ears against the ruler.

4 We found out sound vibrations travel better through wood then through the air.

Lucy

Figure 5.5 Does sound travel better through wood than through air?

Notice how the teacher helped Lucy to write a whole account, by suggesting the function of a cartoon strip (and folding the paper into squares). The format helped her sequence the reporting of the investigation. The importance of this is to recognise that young children find chronological and spatial organisation difficult.

A class of 9 year olds had been working on a project 'Rainbows'. Some of the experimental work had involved using ray-boxes to make spectra and for some, to see how filters affect the way we see. The teacher had asked the children to explain why things are different colours. Notice how this boy has personalised this knowledge, using an everyday word 'bounce' instead of the specialist word 'reflect' which the teacher used in the class. He was comfortable with the word 'absorbed', even though many other children used the word 'trapped'. See Figure 5.6.

Figure 5.6 An explanation of why a car looks blue

A class of 7 to 8 year olds had been experimenting with magnets. The teacher had provided a selection of ferromagnetic and non-ferromagnetic materials and had asked them to find which materials around the school were attracted to magnets. As a means of assessing whether the children could apply their recently acquired knowledge, their teacher read them a story she had written about a little boy called 'Magnetic Magnum.' The boy was trapped inside a suit of armour which became magnetised by an electromagnet. The class was invited to write the penultimate section, describing the boy's adventures, before eventually being removed from the suit of armour. Tom wrote an exciting story, (spelling only corrected):

> That day his dad asked Magnum if he wanted to go to a race track and Magnum said, yes so they went to the biggest one and the poles which hold up the ribbons stuck to him. Then some racing cars came by and Magnum stuck to a racing car and when the man waved the flag at the end of the race it came flying out of the man's hand and went to the car because Magnum had made the car into a magnet too. On the way round the track he screamed for help and the armour rattled about and they used ten tonne weights which stuck to the car. The crane was made of aluminium so it won't stick to it. And the crane with a big hook pulled Magnum off the car and the driver of the racing car was disqualified because the magnet on the car made him go faster. And just then his dad came ranting up and said 'Let's go home.'

Some 10 year olds were working in small groups on activities associated with an electric circuit. One group was given a bayonet fitting light bulb and one with a screw fitting at the end. Each base had been carefully sawn through so that the children could trace the path of the wires. For safety the bulbs were placed in plasticine. They were asked to draw carefully what they could see and write about the reasons for the differences they observed. See Figure 5.7.

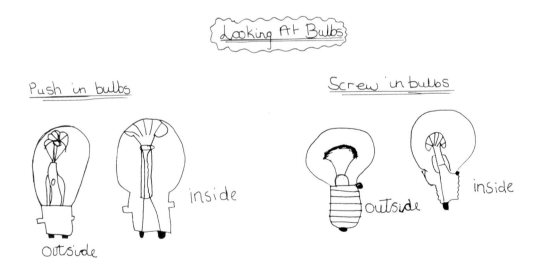

*Figure 5.7* Examining different light bulbs

Anyone with an acquaintance with the process of writing will appreciate that writing is not just communicating, not just a form of representation. It is thinking, learning to think, and in so doing coming to understand. What this section has focused on is the potential of different representations, including writing tasks, to maximise learning. Helping children to be sufficiently confident to choose their own form of representation in science (i.e. to re-present their ideas) is a demanding and effective learning activity for them. However, at the same time it is an effective way for the teacher to assess their understanding.

## ASSESSING WHAT CHILDREN SAY AND DO

The argument put forward is that the more a teacher tries to tap instances of a child's understanding, in terms of speaking and recording, the more complete the picture for assessment. The third dimension is the assessment of a child's performance while doing science. The following example demonstrates this: Matthew and Lee, two 10 year old boys, were working on an investigation: Is skin sensitive all over the body? Their teacher observed the pair, and Figure 5.8 shows her assessment notes.

In discussing their findings, the teacher asked why they thought some areas of skin were more sensitive than others. Lee said that the skin was 'thinner near the nerves', and Matthew added that the 'bones protected the nerves, so things couldn't be felt very easily'. The teacher then asked where the nerves actually were, and their ideas again referred to being 'under skin' (Lee) and 'under bones' (Matthew). The teacher thought that it was appropriate to show a cross-sectional diagram of skin, and then asked all the class to feel their bones and skin on their hands. She used the results obtained by Lee and Matthew to inform the discussion further.

Although the teacher felt that her intervention was appropriate for helping the pair guide their investigation, their overall understanding in class discussion showed misunderstanding. The teacher had assessed their practical capabilities by observation, and then assessed their conceptual understanding through particular questions.

Matthew and Lee had demonstrated their understandings both conceptually and procedurally, and this had been recorded in the teacher's own particular notation. Planning to observe in such a purposeful way is the key to effective assessment. The teacher already had some idea about the pair's performance in scientific investigations, and clearly wanted them to demonstrate this. A dilemma in assessment is illustrated by only Lee providing evidence that the test was unfair. Can one infer that too for Matthew? Or should fair-testing be discussed with Matthew based on this investigation? Or should this part of the science process be analysed at a later date in another investigation? What she did record is shown in Figure 5.8.

## THE LANGUAGE OF THE STATEMENTS OF ATTAINMENT

Assessing Matthew and Lee, using National Curriculum criteria, the teacher felt she had sufficient evidence to record the results shown in Table 5.1.

Mathew and Lee:  | IS skin sensitive all over the body? |

10.35

M - 'pencil point' tries L's arm and hand:

Yes/no for pencil felt    L tests M.

M - 'going too quickly'  L slower.

1:3c? L - 'need to shut your eyes'   Swap M → L

*   Where is this going? What are they actually going to record?!

Me - 'Do you think some areas are more sensitive than others?'
Me - 'Has this pencil point test helped you find this out?'  M and L
                                                              Yes

    M'L says yes.... time it.... skin goes dented'

Me - 'What else can you do?'  Uncertain.
Me - 'How will you actually measure that some areas are
        more sensitive than others?'

    M tries watch → L    no success.
I refer to another groups idea – card and pins.
Advised M and L to select areas - test with pins.

    M → L  pins close / eyes shut.
    M. 'how many can you feel?'   No results recorded.
Me - 'should you write this down?'   M - wrote 1 or 2

                              L - 'draw my skin' (arm and hand)
                              M ⟋ 1 2   5 places on drawing.

    L → M ( M had opened pin distance). L 'not fair.... must be
        ↘ on                                              same'
          drawing different colour         ( 1:3c )
              1  2

                                          Me ⟶
                                        ⌒ ruler?!
11.15
      return
      Drawing – filled with numbers/colours. Confusing – pin distances?
      Asked M and L to sort out and try to compare.   ( M and L 1:2b )
      ① Difficult and needed to retest.

Figure 5.8  A teacher's observation notes

*Table 5.1* Record of Matthew's and Lee's achievements

|          | 1:2b | 1:3b | 1:3c | 1:3d | 2:4a |
|----------|------|------|------|------|------|
| Matthew  | X    | /    | /    | /    | /    |
| Lee      | X    | /    | X    | /    | /    |

*Notes*
/ = experienced.
X = achieved.

From the brief selection of Statements of Attainment for this particular session the teacher was able to justify some achievement, but she felt there was insufficient evidence for understanding the complete process. They would still need to demonstrate an ability to predict (1:2a, 1:3a) and to explain (1:2c, 1:3d) at a later date.

When deciding how she might award a level of attainment for 'knowledge and understanding' to Matthew and Lee, it was important to appreciate the nature of this statement (2:4a: 'be able to name and locate major organs of the human body') in the context of this investigation. The statements have particular requirements, for a child to 'know that', 'know how', 'know about', 'be able to' or 'understand', each produces a different focus for assessment of understanding, as illustrated in the following statements of attainment:

- AT2:2a know that plants and animals need certain conditions to sustain life.
- AT2:5a be able to name and outline the function of major organs and organ systems in mammals and in flowering plants.
- AT2:7a understand the life processes of movement, respiration, growth, reproduction, excretion, nutrition and sensitivity in animals.

The above list demonstrates a progression in understanding, where the language in the Statements of Attainment suggests a sequence of: know that (i.e. recall of knowledge), be able to (i.e. apply this knowledge) and understand (i.e. make connections and have a deeper understanding). Qualter *et al.* (1990) refer to this as a progression in 'quality of understanding'.

ACTIVITY 5.3  PROGRESSION IN QUALITY OF UNDERSTANDING

Select one Attainment Target. Does the quality in understanding follow the sequence, i.e. 'know that', 'be able to' and 'understand'?

What do the statements imply for the assessment of children's understanding?

What types of investigation/activity would help a teacher assess these levels of statements effectively?

Observing what children are doing when they are investigating is demanding and time consuming; the assessment criteria require an appropriate task to match their particular requirements. Other strategies of assessment can be used: asking children specific questions during an investigation, checking their analysis of a story and examining their responses to a pencil and paper test. These three activities, on a common theme of 'Food' are illustrated in Activities 5.4 to 5.6.

### ACTIVITY 5.4  ASSESSING ATTAINMENT TARGET 1 THROUGH QUESTIONING

As an exercise in purposefully trying to think of suitable questions, a group of teachers periodically 'brainstorm' questions that will inform them when assessing children's capabilities of Attainment Target 1 (i.e. process skills). This list was thought up for an investigation about dissolving sugar.

1:1a  (*observe*) What happens to sugar when we add it to water?
1:2a  (*predict*) What will happen if you use another sugar variety?
1:2b  (*related observations*) What happened when you used other sugar varieties?
1:2c  (*conclusion*) Did you expect this to happen?
1:3a  (*predict/everyday experience*) What happens to sugar in a cup of tea?
1:3b  (*measurement*) How will you measure sugar dissolving in tea?
1:3c  (*fair-test*) Did you make sure you used the same amounts of sugar etc.?
1:3d  (*explanation*) Why did the sugar dissolve faster in hotter tea?
1:4a  (*predict/prior knowledge*) How can you make sugar crystals?
1:4b  (*fair-test measurement*) How are you measuring the amount of solution?
1:4c  (*conclusions*) Did you expect to produce crystals from this solution?

Choose another area of science and devise similar questions for assessment purposes.

### ACTIVITY 5.5  SPOT THE PHYSICAL AND CHEMICAL CHANGES

A teacher had been teaching about the differences between physical and chemical changes, over a three week period. The children had had ample opportunity to investigate the differences and talk about both sorts of changes in everyday life. He gave his 10 year olds a story to analyse.
    See the worksheet in Appendix VI – answers at end of this unit.
    Write your own story to assess understanding in an area of science in which your children are working. For younger children consider a pictorial presentation with few words.

### ACTIVITY 5.6  TESTING UNDERSTANDING OF FAIR-TESTING

Over a term, a class of 10 year olds had been investigating the way heat travelled. They were confident in working on their own. The teacher was reading *Charlie and the Chocolate Factory,* and decided to use this setting to give the class a pencil and paper test; he wanted to assess the children's understanding of handling variables to be fair, so that valid conclusions could be drawn.

See the worksheet in Appendix VII.

Create your own worksheet to assess understanding of fair-testing, in an area of science in which your children are working.

## RECORDING CHILDREN'S ACHIEVEMENTS

A teacher cannot hope to record everything in the classroom, but as we have pointed out, the snapshots obtained can be informed snapshots. A careful use of record sheets, devised for a particular purpose can make the task more effective. Mitchell and Koshy (1993) analyse teacher assessment record sheets in all areas of the curriculum, and the one we illustrate, in Figure 5.9, was selected to show the record of a 9 year old. She was assessed while planning how to be fair during a group investigation about the strength of concrete.

The value of this particular format is that the record sheet provides sections to describe features of a teacher's assessment of a child in more detail:

The **possible outcome** focuses the assessment.
The **account** records what happened.
The **interpretation** demonstrates achievements.
The **action** devises the next stages for this particular child.

The authors describe this recording process as a 'minimal framework that can be redesigned to accommodate individual preferences in the light of personal experience' and as a reflection of the 'planning-learning-assessing dynamic'. This type of record therefore not only notes a child's achievements, but also suggests a way forward for learning with the teacher's understandings of that particular child.

 ACTIVITY 5.7  RECORDING TEACHER ASSESSMENT

From the above example of recording teacher assessment, select an appropriate time when teaching, to evaluate this process of gathering and interpreting a child's achievements.

How straightforward is it to predict possible outcomes?
How difficult is it to describe an account of the event?
What decisions have to be made about the interpretation?
Is the action seen as a positive way forward?

In no other area of education is tentativeness in outcomes more obvious and decisions so potentially hazardous than in assessing children's learning. Magdalene Lampert (1985) writes

FORMATIVE TEACHER ASSESSMENT RECORD

Y1 ☐    Y2 ☐    Y3 ☐

Y4 ☑    Y5 ☐    Y6 ☐

Name : ...Eleanor...........................................................    Date : ..................................................................

Activity : ...Which concrete is the strongest? How will we find out?.........................................

| Possible Outcomes |
|---|
| Linking use of concrete to its properties  AT3 : 3a<br>Devising and carrying out a fair test for testing strength of concrete made previously  AT1 : 2b, AT1 : 3b |

| Account | Interpretation | Action |
|---|---|---|
| Discussed physical properties of concrete 'ingredients'. "You need to add water. If you used it for a house it's not suitable, it's too crumbly." Discussed a testable idea, "If you drop them, the lightest will break." Worked through the idea that weight wasn't relevant with the group. Tested strength by dropping masses. Varied height and assisted to see the need for a fair test. Later discussed needing to keep the height the same, "Because it's fair." | 3:3a understands use of concrete as building material.<br><br>1:2a prediction made while trying to isolate variables.<br><br>Attempts at isolating the variable.<br><br>1:2b series of related observations made while testing. | Uses of other building materials, e.g. water-proofing.<br><br>Discuss and evaluate the need for a fair test.<br><br>Further practice devising and carrying out a fair test. |

**Comments :**

Contributed to many parts of the discussion and made many suggestions. Some testable ideas but not able to verbally follow these through. Evidence of understanding fair testing through practical demonstration needed.

*Figure 5.9*  A formative teacher assessment record

with great sensitivity, from a perspective of her own practice, about the difficulty of coming to a solution for a classroom problem, where choices between alternative courses of action seemingly have to be made. In her case the problem was associated with learning and behaviour. Similarly, the real world of assessment poses dilemmas which have to be managed; the task is about balancing decisions, about coping rather than solving, for assessment of children's understanding has no clear cut solutions.

## SUMMARY

This unit has examined the 'snapshot' evidence available for children's learning in science within the classroom. Using what the child says, does and records as a basis for gathering this evidence, an example of a teacher assessment sheet is given to help formalise the recording of achievements. This interpreted information provides a means for planning learning objectives and future classroom action.

## ANSWERS TO ACTIVITY 5.5

*Physical changes*
Starched white cloth
Dissolving Aspirin tablet
Cut stems
Element glowing red
Sliced mushrooms
Kettle boiling
Smashed cup
Cracked open egg
Dissolved sugar
Melted butter
Tearing up bits of paper
Kettle boiling

*Chemical changes*
Bacon cooking
Egg white colour change
Milk curdled
Burnt toast

# Attitudes towards science teaching and towards science

It is not the intention of this unit to deal with how pupils develop an attitude to science: of responsibility, cooperation, perseverance, open-mindedness and so on. Rather we wish to consider the significance of attitude in teachers' thinking, essentially how you 'feel' towards teaching science and towards science as a subject.

In the first unit it was stated that an accepted knowledge base for teaching science consisted of an understanding of subject matter for teaching and of the way children learn. To these two components needs to be added a third, a teacher's *attitude* to the subject. Why should there be such interest in a teacher's attitude to science? The argument is that implicit beliefs and attitudes guide planning and a teacher's action in the classroom. Smith and Neale (1991) provide a very useful summary of researchers who have shown the way attitudes frame teachers' work and shape their decisions and practice.

So it's not so much knowing about 'philosophy', but rather knowing about how reviewing your attitudes (feelings), may have a considerable effect on what science you do in class, and how you do it.

## ATTITUDE TOWARDS SCIENCE TEACHING

Bennett and Carré (1993) used three imaginary teachers' 'portraits' in their research, to find out about an individual's attitude to teaching and learning science. These portraits are shown in Activity 6.1 where you are invited to check your own attitude; they incorporate ideas about the nature of science and about teaching and learning.

 ACTIVITY 6.1  ATTITUDE TO SCIENCE TEACHING

Think about your attitude to science, and the assumptions you have about learning and teaching the subject. Identify with *one or more* of the three 'portraits', A, B or C.

## Teacher A

'Science is "hands-on" practical work, discovering the world around us using all five senses. Initiatives are by pupils; they pose the questions and I encourage them to work independently. I refrain from giving them clues or science information to help their enquiry. I don't mind if the pupils use descriptive, non-scientific language.'

## Teacher B

'Science is a collection of laws, an accurate and organised body of knowledge. I present content very clearly and direct practical work to prevent aimless activity. Essentially the children gather relevant information and confirm for themselves what are already laid down as core concepts. We always use correct scientific language.'

## Teacher C

'Science is a creation of human mind; truth is formed in the mind of the observer. I assume that pupils have extensive knowledge about their world and I help them apply and relate what they already know to new problems. I challenge them to reject, reshape or extend their ideas and to justify why they think the way they do. I encourage them to use scientific language when explaining.'

How did you fare? Notice that we did not ask you to make a choice between the three, but rather to indicate how each might represent your feeling. The general picture which emerged in our research was that attitudes were favourably inclined towards a practical, problem-solving approach to science teaching and to a constructivist stance to learning. The most significant result was that we were provided with an idea of the *balance* of teaching strategies that individuals thought they would use. It is important to think of teachers having a variety of approaches, to satisfy different ages and abilities, and different aims with respect to teaching science to the National Curriculum.

These findings are particularly interesting in the light of the discussion document by Alexander *et al.* (1992). In reviewing available evidence about the quality of classroom practice they emphasised that, too often, the debate about practice was conducted in terms of a simplistic dichotomy, between 'traditional' and 'progressive', or 'formal' and 'informal'. The balance between the different organisational strategies to which they referred were not mutually exclusive; effective science teaching can result from a mix of the approaches described by Teachers A and C, with some use of the teacher directed strategies of Teacher B. Wolfe (1989) provides one of the few accounts of the way ideas about the nature of science were conveyed to children in a science lesson. By monitoring the teacher's behaviour, she gathered 'clues' about the particular nature of science being conveyed; her analytical scheme contained some of the practical criteria which appear in Activity 6.2. Observing teachers teaching is a very demanding exercise and analysis of 'clues' is time consuming. However the suggested pointers of what to observe in Activity 6.2 will be useful as a focus, to check some of your assumptions about how you teach science and the messages you inadvertently convey.

## ACTIVITY 6.2  TAKING A CLOSER LOOK AT MYSELF TEACHING SCIENCE

Some primary schools provide time for the science coordinator to visit other teachers in their classrooms. If another person cannot observe you, use a tape recorder and listen to parts of your lesson later. The characteristics of the three 'portraits' will help focus questions about your actions.

### Teacher A (seen as a 'problem solver') is characterised by:
- encouraging children to be autonomous and to work independently
- helping children to ask productive questions
- offering initiatives to children
- refraining from giving clues or science information to children
- providing motivating material for 'hands-on' enquiry

### Teacher B (teacher dominated style, acting as a 'verifier' of information) is characterised by:
- transmitting content clearly within a 'framework' provided by the teacher
- thinking mainly about product. Providing clear tasks by which to produce it
- preventing aimless activity by directing investigations
- showing and demonstrating
- scientific vocabulary purposefully incorporated into lessons

### Teacher C (personal and social) is characterised by:
- negotiating understanding and helping pupils to reshape their knowledge
- planning for pupils' misconceptions
- challenging pupils to predict, explain and justify their use of evidence
- providing ways of applying new concepts
- eliciting ideas by setting up dialogues

1. How would you describe the characteristics of your teaching? What *balance* do you achieve, as a mix of the three? For what reasons does the balance shift?
2. How do your *intentions* (your planning) match your performance?

---

## ATTITUDE TOWARDS THE NATURE OF SCIENCE

A positive attitude towards the nature of scientific activity is seen to be vital for the impact on classroom behaviours of teachers. The dangers of children acquiring inert bodies of content knowledge are well known and even though the National Curriculum emphasises the importance of process, or procedural knowledge, there is still a temptation for the unsure teacher to neglect enquiry approaches. Cleminson (1990) argues that a problem for teachers arises from the fact that the nature of science has been re-evaluated by philosophers over the past 30 years, and science curricula have not kept pace with contemporary views. Many of us are struggling with a hundred years of tradition. Take a few moments to check in Activity 6.3, if *you* are! Your responses to the statements can later be examined from the text of this unit.

I.M. MARSH LIBRARY LIVERPOOL L17 6BD
TEL. 0151 231 5216/5299

## ACTIVITY 6.3  HOW SURE ARE YOU ABOUT IDEAS ABOUT SCIENCE?

How do you feel about these statements? Record your response on the right.

*Agree*                    *Not so sure*

1.  Science is special and distinct from other subject disciplines.
2.  Western science is distinctive, and more valid than science of other cultures.
3.  Facts are definitely facts, they are objective. You can't have two contradictory descriptions of the same thing.
4.  Observation and inference mean the same thing.
5.  Science knowledge affects what we observe.
6.  Only science hypotheses can be proved absolutely.
7.  All scientific theories are proven and do not need to be tested any more.
8.  Imagination has no place in developing science theory, for it is based on reasoning and experimental techniques.
9.  Astrology, acupuncture and medicine are science.

(*Note*: an excellent article, by Ryan and Aikenhead (1992), gives examples of questionnaires on the nature of science, and in particular the way technology and science interact.)

One persistent idea about science is the belief that scientists are objective in their observations, and make judgements about information obtained through the senses in an unbiased manner. This is not so. Our lives are possible only because we have *personal* theories about what the world is like, and our knowledge is built up as an accumulation of experiences. Our observations are theory dependent. Claxton (1984) puts it this way:

Common sense says we see things the way they are, then we make decisions about what's important, and finally we select actions that will get us what we want and avoid what we don't. Common sense is wrong. What we see is an output of our personal theory, not an input of it.

So we have to learn to interpret what we see, and because the world is always changing and we are changing, we have to adjust constantly and rethink our theories. A good example of how theories are imaginative constructions of the mind is to look at the two maps in Figure 6.1; just two ways of representing the same data.

The deficiencies of the traditional Mercator projection (e.g. Greenland's representation is 3/4 the size of North America and polar regions do not exist) are corrected in the Peter's projection where surface areas are more accurately represented. However the Peter's projection also has its shortcomings, in distortions of shape and directional inaccuracies. Our understanding of the relative sizes of the countries and the position of Europe in relation to the rest of the world is governed by a particular way of representing data. For example, which map would you choose to check that Europe (9.7 million sq. kilometres) is smaller than South America (17.8 million sq. kilometres)? Which is best for navigation? Both maps work, but neither represent an 'absolute truth'.

A scientific parallel can be found in the traditional representation of light as wave-like ripples on water. The theory explains many properties of light, but the results of more recent experiments on light cannot be explained in this way. A second theory explains light behaviour as if it were composed of particles. The theories explain different phenomena, but neither is true in any absolute sense. White (1988) makes a further point, stressing that the models are simply convenient ways of demonstrating reflection and other properties of light, 'they do not really explain why light behaves as it does, they merely show how some of the phenomena of light can be simulated'.

Cleminson focuses on the shift in thinking about what science is all about, and suggests that the 'new' philosophy of science, if brought to bear on science educational practice, would incorporate the following assumptions:

1. Scientific knowledge is tentative and should never be equated with truth. It has only temporary status.
2. There can be no sharp distinction between observation and inference. Our observations are not objective, but are governed by our experiences; we view the world through theoretical lenses built up from prior knowledge.
3. New knowledge in science is produced by creative acts of the imagination allied with the methods of scientific enquiry. As such, science is a personal and immensely human activity. It is not value free.
4. Acquisition of new scientific knowledge is problematic and never easy. Abandoning cherished knowledge that has been falsified usually occurs with reluctance.
5. Scientists study a world of which they are a part, not a world from which they are apart. There is a social context and social accountability to science.

Thus the view of science as an impersonal and unproblematic study must be discarded; also the notion that observation is a neutral activity, for there is a very human and social aspect to its study. To emphasise the point, Medawar (1982) purposely exaggerates two conceptions of the nature of the scientific activity. In the first, which he describes as the 'romantic' conception, truth takes shape in the mind of the observer, whereas in the 'worldly' view truth lies in nature, and is to be got at only through the evidence of the senses. The two portrayals contradict, but as Medawar explains:

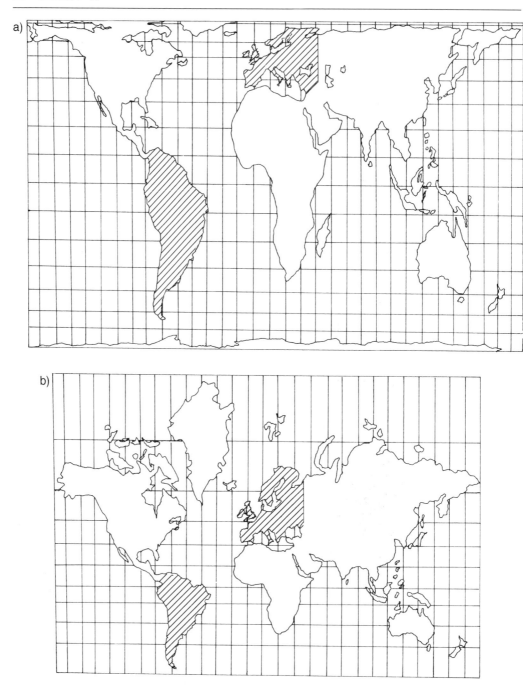

a)  The Peter's projection (first drawn in 1977)      b)  Mercator's projection (first drawn in 1569)

*Figure 6.1* Two ways of representing the same mapping data

There is no paradox here: it just happens that what are usually thought of as two alternative and indeed competing accounts of one process of thought are in fact accounts of *two* successive and complementary episodes of thought that occur in every advance of scientific understanding.

Medawar describes the process of investigating as, 'having an idea', or raising a hypothesis (an imaginative and creative act of mind) and 'testing it out' (a ruthless critical process of enquiry). In practice, because of the rapid reciprocation of 'guesswork and checkwork', to use Medawar's famous phrase, the distinctions are blurred. If the invented world of the hypothesis bears no resemblance to reality when tested, then the hypothesis is wrong and needs modification. This idea of tentativeness is particularly important in school where a teacher may believe that science offers irrevocably true statements.

The very personal act of 'doing science' causes problems, for as previously pointed out (see Unit 3), making sense of phenomena can create 'alternative frameworks' which may conflict with public knowledge. This mismatch can happen at any age. There is a second consequence to the personal aspect of science knowledge. Science is not dogma and Ziman (1980), more than most writers, has stressed the social dimension, where influences of the political, economic and moral attitudes of those in power frequently alter progress in science. (The story of how the whole social network of people and resources influenced the discovery of pulsars at Cambridge in 1968 is unfolded lucidly by Woolgar, 1988.) Progress in science may not be as impartial and rational as one is lead to believe!

Summing up, this brief consideration of the nature of science emphasises that science:

- is tentative, and nothing can be proved absolutely; a theory is provisional;
- is subjective, several accounts of the same event may exist side by side;
- involves the use of both imagination and critical enquiry;
- theory can be disproved by testing, a well established theory can be demolished with a single observation;
- is a very human enterprise and its progress is influenced by social pressures.

These ideas of Cleminson do not mean that in science 'anything goes', that the nature of science is some myth, and that the philosophy of science, as Paul Feyerabend (1975) has described it is 'a poorly understood form of insanity'. Certainly there are many examples of 'real-world' routine science which do not, and great discoveries which have not, conformed to the procedures which we refer to as 'the scientific method'. But that does not mean that the nature of science, should not be embedded in our teaching strategies at primary level. The challenge is to introduce children to procedures of investigation; the essential character of the scientific exercise can be practised for *some* of the time, along with other science activities, as discussed in other units. The practical perspective involves children in asking questions, carrying out investigations, interpreting results and so on, reflecting some of the procedures used by scientists, which philosophers like Karl Popper (1959) have tried to define.

Figure 6.2 gives a representation of what that may look like, with a class of 7 year olds. In autumn the class collected, sorted by weight (5–20g) and stored the fruits of the horse chestnut.

**Stage 1**

They discussed what they had heard about the different ways of hardening conkers to make 'the best' or the 'champion' conker. Accounts were read of competitions and anecdotal tales were told. In other words, experience, myths and intuitive ideas were examined. The question posed was, 'Is there a secret to getting a champion conker?'

**Stage 2**

They raised hypotheses, as possible explanations for testing, about which recipe (treatment) was the best for hardening conkers. The favourite ideas for testing were; soaking conkers in vinegar and water, baking in the oven, boiling and freezing them. The children's experiences at home were foremost in their reasoning, as these statements, taken from a lengthy transcript, show:

Ian.    *Because when you put it in the freezer, if you leave it there for about two hours, the ice goes inside it and gets harder.*

Ben.    *'cos if you leave it out there for two nights and you get up and put more boiling water in, it will like evaporate, and get really hard.* (He mentioned in a disjointed fashion that when food boiled dry it formed a hard mass.)

Daniel.    *I want to baking it because when cakes get baked they get bigger and stronger.* (Perhaps his experience of eating cakes played a part in this causal relationship!)

Victoria.    *Because soaking it in vinegar and water might make it bigger and stronger, because it will have two treatments, two things put in it.*

A histogram showing the results of a survey on the four predictions indicated that there was disagreement, and a genuine conflict to resolve (the teacher used the word hypothesis as an untested statement, to guide the investigation. A statement which after practical testing was being found reliable, could *then* be called a theory).

**Stage 3**

The hypotheses for testing the basic question, 'Which treatment was the best for hardening conkers?' were based on a causal relationship, e.g. 'If conkers are baked then they will get (stronger) harder'.

The children designed and made 'conker bonkers' to test the hardness of the treated conkers. The chosen design was a kilogram mass, dropped from a height onto the conker; a scale gave a measure of the height from which the mass dropped. The control variables were vigorously debated; in particular they had to agree how to identify a successful 'bonk'. This was important, for the success of the investigation to a large extent hinged on the children's ability to judge a crack of 1 mm! Such a conker failed the test.

**Stage 4**

There was no doubt in the mind of this class! The investigations indicated that the best treatment for hardening conkers was freezing them, and the best size was the smallest, 0.5 g and below. They had disproved three hypotheses, but through their testing, with large samples of conkers, they were willing to rely on the theory that the hardest conkers had had the frozen treatment.

Philosophers such as Popper would insist that at no time could the children's (or any) theory be *proven*. One can never be certain, no matter how many observations are made, and theories cannot be tested to prove them to be true. However the class teacher accepted that these 7 year olds had 'proved their theory' and was not troubled with Popper's suggestion that theories could only be shown to be false (Figure 6.2). The majority of teachers are

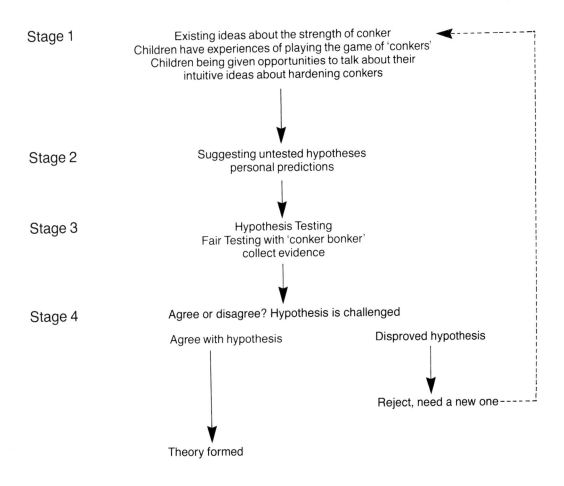

Stage 1    Existing ideas about the strength of conker
Children have experiences of playing the game of 'conkers'
Children being given opportunities to talk about their
intuitive ideas about hardening conkers

Stage 2    Suggesting untested hypotheses
personal predictions

Stage 3    Hypothesis Testing
Fair Testing with 'conker bonker'
collect evidence

Stage 4    Agree or disagree? Hypothesis is challenged

Agree with hypothesis    Disproved hypothesis

Reject, need a new one

Theory formed

*Figure 6.2* Popper's view of science: a teacher's interpretation

content with 'proving' rather than 'disproving' a theory. The point is an academic one, for as Woolgar (1988) has pointed out:

> It has become clear that both verification and falsification suffer from the weakness of the central assumption that observations are neutral: little attention is given to the way in which observations bear upon the statement (generalization) at issue. In the classic example of the generalization 'all swans are white', it may be logically more attractive to attempt its falsification than its verification, but both approaches pay scant regard to the issue of what is to count as a 'swan' or 'white'. Is a swan dipped in soot to count as a white swan really?

There is certainly no need to explain to children the essential steps in this method of science thinking, in any explicit fashion. The main reason for this is that the suggested sequence may be a philosopher's dream for a tidy structure. There is no such thing as *the* scientific method. As Medawar points out, 'scientists observe its rules unconsciously and do not understand it in the sense of being able to put it clearly into words'.

But that should not imply that attitudes to the nature of science teaching and the nature of science are trivial issues. As Smith and Neale have shown, attitudes frame your work; how you view the discipline will shape the messages you give to children about the processes involved in 'doing science', just as surely as the messages given about caring for living things, about conservation and pollution. Also, the messages you give to children about what science is *not*, may be just as important as messages about what it is.

## SUMMARY

Much research has shifted its focus from identifying effective actions of teachers to the study of the knowledge and attitude that underlie those classroom actions. It has been shown that teachers' beliefs and attitude toward the nature of science, and about how the subject should be taught and learned, all play a significant role in how teachers teach. The way you think about contemporary views of the nature of science as a discipline, and the way you interpret the list of assumptions described by Cleminson will alter the way you plan, the teaching strategies you use and the way you respond to children.

# It's not fair!

If you use *The Daily Fib* as a model, it is important to give the children in your class ample opportunity to talk about each section. You can also back up the point being made, by providing examples of misleading statements from current newspapers. For example:

1. Looking at 'Spuds Lead to Crime', get the children to find examples of stories which show correlation of two items but not necessarily a cause and effect relationship. One 10 year old girl was inspired to write an article for their newspaper, 'Socks Cause Nits'; she started by saying 'I questioned 45 people who had nits. They all wear socks . . .'

2. The advert 'Nine Out of Ten Film Stars Use Scrubbo Soap' is readily seen as misleading. Children see that the sample is very small, only nine out of ten, not nine out of every ten as they are led to believe. Children found this true, but misleading, statement easy to understand and could create their own versions. The teacher had to explain more carefully what qualifications were needed in adverts to be called a 'film star', or an 'expert' or to be 'famous'! And what does 'use' mean? (One child wrote: 'when it said *use* Scrubbo soap they might not wash with it they might take their rings off with it, and if it smells they might put it in the loo.')

3. Children found the words 'up to' the most commonly misleading phraseology in newspapers. They were found to be particularly associated with expected salary, (up to £30,000 p.a. . . .) and in advertising reductions on premiums on car insurance, (up to 30 per cent if your car is over 2 years old).

4. Looking at 'Your Stars' caused considerable debate! Horoscopes are taken seriously by many children and their parents as reliable predictions of future events. One teacher collected a variety of horoscopes and looked carefully at the language; the way the predictions were unspecific, the basic advice given and the contradictions in different magazines and newspapers. Children found it easy to invent horoscopes:

*Aries* Your week will be peaceful and relaxing. You will be reunited with an old friend. Romance – it will be a quiet week for you. Health – look after your face.

5.   One teacher encouraged her class to write down what they thought was misleading; a 9 year old spotted this:

> *The Daily Fib* misled us by saying Hottest Tuesday the 14th July for 7 years when the last Tuesday on the 14th July was 7 years ago. There is only 1 Tuesday on the 14th of July in 7 years.

6.   Descriptions of the same event written by different people with a different perspective created a lively discussion about the way news is manipulated and evidence presented. Controversial issues such as fox hunting and seal culling were topics discussed and children found no difficulty in creating their own stories, some serious and some comic. One teacher listening in to a group of 11 year olds overheard them discussing, 'Well what *is* a fact?'

In two schools where this programme was used the teachers followed the newspaper work with a series of sessions on the difficulty of setting up a truly fair-test.

# A personal 'journey' in understanding electricity

A personal progression in understanding electricity was traced by a teacher who was eager to tackle his misconceptions within this conceptual area. He realised early on in his career that a deeper understanding was needed for him to be able to represent these concepts to children in the most appropriate way. The following is a diagrammatic representation of that teacher's progression in understanding over the ten years since leaving teacher training (Figure App.1):

## His story

His story can be explained as follows. His educational background was essentially scientific; 'O' levels, 'A' levels and a degree in chemistry would appear excellent qualifications for teaching science. His knowledge of electricity allowed him to describe quite complex experimental procedures (e.g. an electron gun) but this description and acceptance of these 'true' situations overrode the necessary need to question what was really going on. The basic understanding of what constitutes the simple circuit process was missing; he knew electrons were involved as the experiments in physics demonstrated, but to analyse this phenomena any deeper did not occur to him. The exam results illustrated his success in remembering high level facts that in reality had many gaps.

The need to gain a greater understanding of electricity developed while teaching in a primary school. The 10 year old children in his class were given worksheets to set up simple circuits instructing them to make switches and light bulbs in different situations, e.g. traffic lights. If any questions came up about what was going on inside the battery or wires the children were alerted to reference books which invariably gave them difficult explanations. Any further questions they asked, which may have stemmed from the reference books, were answered by 'you don't need to know that yet'. Consequently the written work produced by the children was relatively poor while at the same time his confidence in his once secure

I.M. MARSH LIBRARY LIVERPOOL L17 6BD
TEL. 0151 231 5216/5299

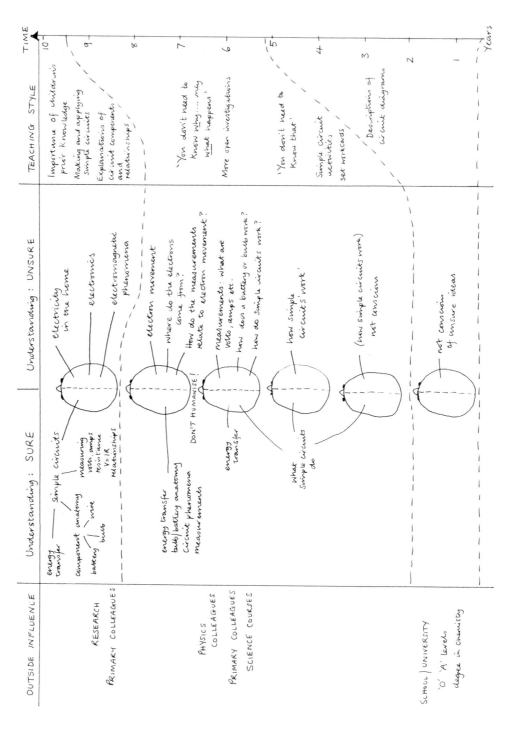

Figure App.1  One teacher's progression in understanding the concept of electricity

understanding of electricity began to dwindle. For a while this confidence drop was lifted by going on science courses where the course organisers stated that the actual doing of the circuitry was more important than knowing what was going on. With this new direction in his teaching and armed with lots of ideas he continued with renewed vigour to teach electricity. He allowed children to make circuits and apply these to different contexts, e.g. burglar alarms, without the use of worksheets. The science in his classroom was fun and rewarding. However the worries returned. He had now become a science coordinator and the introduction of the National Curriculum ensured that science was available to all children. He had many amongst the school staff who were very unconfident about teaching the subject. By setting up staff workshops he demonstrated to the staff the activities in electricity he found particularly useful, illustrating this with children's work. He carefully set out the activities for the teachers to try themselves. While busily occupied in these electricity work-shops the questions began: 'Why does the battery only work when the wires are attached?', 'What's inside the battery?', 'Does the electricity leak out?', 'Why does the bulb light up?'. The answers he gave to their questions were half-remembered versions of his school days. He realised he couldn't properly answer these very valid questions. Again reference books were too complicated and let him down.

The teachers around him had a smattering of knowledge and between them they were able to piece together some of the answers: 'The chemicals inside the battery only work when the wires are connected so electricity doesn't leak', 'The metal inside the bulb gets hot and glows'. All of these explanations were acceptable but they provoked further questioning which led him again to feeling unconfident. The need for his colleagues to know the answers and feel confident themselves was real!

The local secondary school had a good relationship with this primary school and so he set up meetings with the physics staff to sort out some of the difficulties. The explanations were technical but thorough. He had heard of the terms used back in his own school days but the explanations still didn't quite help him make the necessary connections in his own mind. He realised he needed to go far deeper into the atomic structure of the circuit to really develop his understanding. This threw up a lot of other problems; the connections between physics and chemistry had never really been explicit but now they were becoming more noticeable. He had to purposely combine them with the help of the secondary staff. He continued to ask questions and it was on another science course that one large misconception was analysed. The course tutor had explained the flow of electrons as a necklace of beads being pushed round; the electrons were in the wires already (an obvious link with chemistry that he didn't make!) and not pumped out by the battery.

Running further workshops of his own helped him further analyse the need for scientific knowledge in being able to explain phenomena. He found it necessary to bring together all he knew about electricity and understand the many misconceptions children and teachers may have; he became alerted to these throughout any work on electricity. This development in his thinking also led him to look at the research done in this area and readings began to influence further development. For example, teaching about the internal system of the bulb so children can develop explanations about the flow of electricity through the bulb.

He then began to think that the whole circuit needed dissecting; what about the internal system of the battery? What is special about the material used for making wires? He now felt he was analysing the activities he was providing in electricity rather than blindly selecting

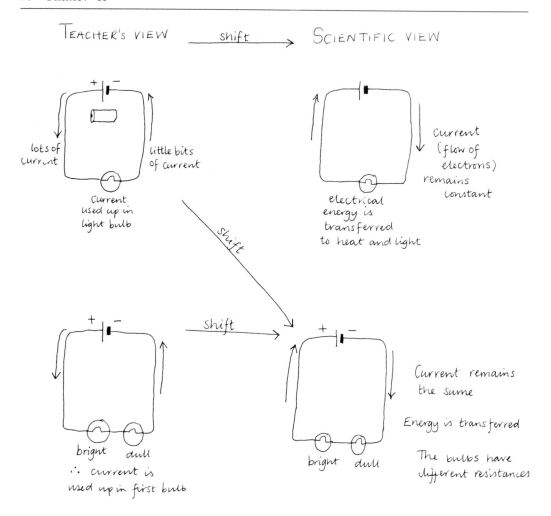

TEACHER'S VIEW _____ shift ____→ SCIENTIFIC VIEW

*Figure App.2* One teacher's understanding of simple circuits as opposed to the scientific view

activities for the children to do. He realised the importance of subject matter knowledge and the clear explanations he needed to provide for the progression in his children's understanding. He had also come to realise how intensely personal his understanding of electricity (and everything else!) was and that by analysing previous experiences, prior knowledge and providing a sociable learning environment the progression in his children's understanding could be made a lot smoother.

What is clear from the 'story' is that outside influences played a large part in the teacher's understanding or confusion in electricity. The way the concepts had been represented to him had a big influence on the way he viewed his ideas in electricity. For example, when a new concept was presented, he felt there was great difficulty in shifting to any new view because of misconceptions he previously had; we can perhaps add the likelihood of previous

instructional representation 'mismatches'. This can be illustrated by the teacher's understanding of simple circuits. The 'everyday' idea he once had about the process involved in
lighting bulbs was very resistant and he would automatically return to an idea which
prevented any further development in understanding. Continued experiences in simple
circuits confused rather than helped! (Figure App.2)

Ideally, teaching should develop children's ideas by avoiding the incidences when the
child returns to previous misconceptions. Teaching should involve simplicity and accuracy of
instructional representations to develop a sequence of deeper thinking. The above example of
the teacher's deepening understanding of electricity would undoubtedly be very different
from a colleague's. Children are exactly the same. A balance in teaching strategies and a
variety of instructional representations is even more important when recognising an
individual's progression in understanding.

# 'Productive' and 'unproductive' questions

Examples of questions, in the context of forces and energy, to illustrate features in Activity 3.2.

## PRODUCTIVE QUESTIONS

These questions have a clear purpose, essentially to promote investigation. The National Curriculum non-statutory guidance gives examples of this type: to review ideas, to demand detailed observation, to justify an idea and so on.

### (Attention getting)

- Have you noticed that all the cars do not go the same distance?
- What have you noticed about the wheels of these cars?
- What do you think is inside the car that makes it move?

### (Measuring and providing data)

- How far does this car go?
- Does the slope make any difference?

### (Comparison and ordering)

- Do you mean that all the cars go the same distance?
- What have we found out about how this car moves?

**(Investigation)**

- Who has the best design for a car?
- Can you think how you can make this car go further?
- Can you think of a way to make this car go only 1 m along the floor?
- Will the wind up car go further if we increase the number of 'winds'?
- Is there a relationship between the size of the car and the distance it travels?

## UNPRODUCTIVE QUESTIONS

Remember that these questions are often used to try to find out what children know, their level of attainment and the degree of their understanding or misunderstanding. The National Curriculum non-statutory guidance makes this clear, 'For teachers and children alike an important part of questioning is the willingness to work to some kind of an answer.'

- What is a force?
- What makes things fall?
- Is force the same as energy?
- Which surfaces are rubbing together to make friction?
- In everyday life, what ways do we use to reduce friction?
- Why does the car slow down?
- How many different types of forces can you see in the classroom?
- What sort of energy is being used to make the car go?

# Questions for science activity

Class                                              Year Group

Term  1a  1b  2a  2b  3a  3b                       Topic

## Activities

Attention
Focusing
questions

- - - - - - - - - - - - - - - - - - - - - - - - - - - - - - - - - - - - - - - - - -

Measuring/
Counting
questions

- - - - - - - - - - - - - - - - - - - - - - - - - - - - - - - - - - - - - - - - - -

Comparison
questions

- - - - - - - - - - - - - - - - - - - - - - - - - - - - - - - - - - - - - - - - - -

Action
questions

- - - - - - - - - - - - - - - - - - - - - - - - - - - - - - - - - - - - - - - - - -

Problem-posing
questions

- - - - - - - - - - - - - - - - - - - - - - - - - - - - - - - - - - - - - - - - - -

Class 4C                                Year Group 8-9 year olds

Term 1a 1b 2a 2b (3a) 3b                Topic The wizard of Oz
                                               Colour and light

## Activities

Attention
Focusing      Do transparent objects make shadows?
questions

- - - - - - - - - - - - - - - - - - - - - - - - - - - - - - - - - - -

Measuring/     How does your shadow change length
Counting
questions      during the day?

- - - - - - - - - - - - - - - - - - - - - - - - - - - - - - - - - - -

Comparison     How do the colours change when you
questions      look through different coloured filters?

- - - - - - - - - - - - - - - - - - - - - - - - - - - - - - - - - - -

Action         What happens when you spin colours?
questions

- - - - - - - - - - - - - - - - - - - - - - - - - - - - - - - - - - -

Problem-posing  How can you make the colours of
questions          the rainbow?

- - - - - - - - - - - - - - - - - - - - - - - - - - - - - - - - - - -

# What's worth writing about in science?

## 1. 'Small-step' writing: learning to write a full report

*Before the investigation*

- Draw a large outline of a head. Write inside all you know about the topic to be investigated.
- Using an overhead projector, write notes for what another group has to investigate.
- Rewrite the title of the investigation in the form of a question.
- Write a list of variables to be controlled.

*During the investigation*

- Label a diagram, provided by the teacher, and write a suitable caption for it.

*After the investigation*

- Write in sentences what a table or graph says of the results.
- Write down one way in which a set of results differs from a previous year's effort.
- Write down suggestions as to how another group's investigation might be improved.
- Complete one part of a report of an investigation (remainder written by the teacher).

## 2. Writing to understand the science which has been done

- Write an expanded report from the meagre information provided in a newspaper article.

- Write a playlet of an important historical event. (The teacher provides key statements on cards.)
- Write some science notes for someone who is preparing a biography of a famous person.
- Rewrite a small part of a textbook.
- Picture in the mind what it would be like to be inside a plant or animal and describe what you can see.
- Write the advertising text on the side of a box containing a science object, persuading the public of its value.
- Write the text to a wordless picture book (published, or pictures collected by the teacher).
- Write an explanation for a comic strip joke/cartoon (see for example those in Johnson, K. (1991) *Physics for You*, Cheltenham: Stanley Thornes).
- Write about one important change observed along the nature trail.
- Make a list of reasons for holding a point of view, e.g. a controversial issue about killing seals. Then in role-play, use the notes to argue the case for it. Use a strategy so that each group decides which devices most effectively suit specific purposes e.g.:

    - appeal to tradition and experience;
    - appeal to reason and common sense;
    - appeal to analogy;
    - appeal to emotions;
    - appeal to experimental evidence.

- Explain why a child's account (an alternative conception) is at odds with what they have just been taught.
- Rewrite the school menu, using newly found knowledge about the constituents of food.
- Present a report to the school governors on how energy could be saved in the school.
- Advise the head teacher on how much water is used in the school each week.
- Explain how you got your estimates.
- Prepare a sequence of instructions on what to do in an investigation, for younger children.
- Send letters and reports, via electronic mailboxes to schools in other parts of the world.

# Story for Activity 5.3

Your task is to spot the physical and chemical changes which occur in the story. Underline them in two different coloured pencils. Afterwards you might like to write a similar story containing hidden changes.

*Mothers' Day Treat*

It was Mothers' Day and Juliette got up very early to treat her mother to a special breakfast in bed. She prepared a large tray with a beautiful white starched cloth, and even a small vase of flowers. The previous night she had cut the bottom of the stems and placed them in water with an Aspirin tablet; her Dad told her the chemicals in the tablet were good for keeping the flowers fresh looking.

She turned on the switch on the cooker, watched the element glow red and placed a large frying pan onto the ring. Two rashers of bacon were soon cooking and sizzling in the fat, together with some mushrooms she had sliced carefully. She cracked open an egg straight into the pan and watched the white change colour as it cooked.

Meanwhile the water in the kettle was boiling, so she made a pot of tea. As usual she was trying to go too quickly, the cup slipped from her fingers and smashed to the floor into little pieces. Juliette hoped her mother hadn't heard the noise!

Almost ready now. She poured the tea, but as she poured the milk she saw it had curdled. 'Oh bother,' she exclaimed. 'Perhaps mummy will like tea without milk today,' she thought, as she stirred in some sugar. She popped two slices of bread into the toaster and whilst waiting, put the cooked food on to the plate. The toast was only slightly burnt in the corner and there wasn't time to make more; the blobs of butter melted quickly.

Juliette had made her mother a card, the picture made from tearing up little bits of coloured paper. She placed it on the tray. What a start to the day!

(Answers given at the end of Unit 5.)

# Appendix VII

# Understanding fair-testing

The class was reading *Charlie and the Chocolate Factory*. They were finding out if they could make chocolate, *quickly*. For their science activity, three pairs of children investigated whether it was better to use margarine or butter. Here are their findings.

Their hypothesis: margarine melts quicker than butter because it is softer.

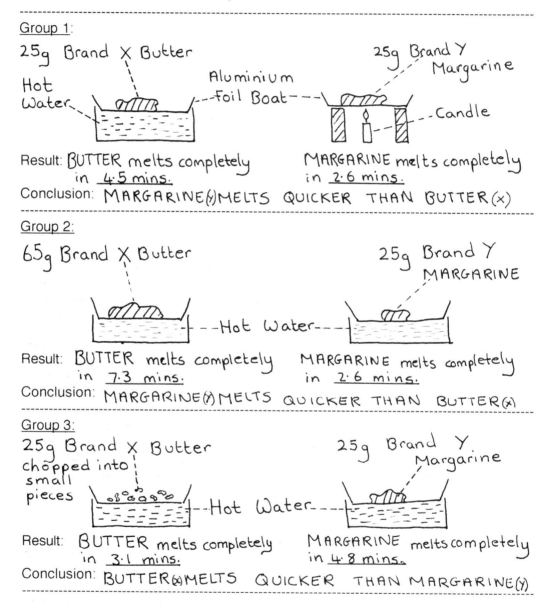

Group 1:

25g Brand X Butter

Hot Water

Aluminium Foil Boat

25g Brand Y Margarine

Candle

Result: BUTTER melts completely in 4.5 mins.

MARGARINE melts completely in 2.6 mins.

Conclusion: MARGARINE (y) MELTS QUICKER THAN BUTTER (x)

Group 2:

65g Brand X Butter

25g Brand Y MARGARINE

Hot Water

Result: BUTTER melts completely in 7.3 mins.

MARGARINE melts completely in 2.6 mins.

Conclusion: MARGARINE (y) MELTS QUICKER THAN BUTTER (x)

Group 3:

25g Brand X Butter chopped into small pieces

25g Brand Y Margarine

Hot Water

Result: BUTTER melts completely in 3.1 mins.

MARGARINE melts completely in 4.8 mins.

Conclusion: BUTTER (x) MELTS QUICKER THAN MARGARINE (y)

Can you advise them on the way they should proceed to make their investigation a fair test?

# Glossary

**Alternative frameworks:** Children of primary and secondary age and beyond hold plausible ideas about the natural world that run counter to the more accepted adult scientific ideas. They are given different labels, including alternative frameworks, children's science, alternative conceptions and mini-theories. Characteristically these ideas are firmly held despite scientific views being offered in teaching. Conceptual change teaching recognises these alternative views.

**Concept:** Is an idea of a class of objects, many interconnected ideas organised to give an understanding of the whole. Most areas of human understanding may be analysed into hierarchies of concepts of ever increasing degrees of abstraction. A simple example is: 'Copper', horse, mammal, vertebrate, chordate. Children and adults construct different concepts (e.g. of force and energy) and therefore inhabit different mental worlds.

**Conceptual change teaching:** Teaching strategies used purposefully to alter children's thinking; for example encouraging them to reflect on their existing ideas, and offering them different ideas from their own, with time to test them out. For example, children may over time, understand that plants do not feed from the soil, but manufacture food through photosynthesis.

**Conceptual understanding (knowledge):** Is concerned with the concepts of science; knowing about generalised ideas such as energy, gravity and heredity.

**Constructivism:** Is a theory of learning, based on personal construct psychology. Individuals do not merely 'take in' new ideas, but are actively and progressively involved in constructing personal meaning. Teaching with this theory in mind requires strategies that enable learners to re-structure their existing knowledge. Teachers need to be aware of an individual's prior knowledge and also the fact that context influences performance only in terms of an individual's perception of it.

**Generative learning model:** Stresses the importance of a learner's prior knowledge and recognises the active construction of meaning. It is taken to be synonymous to constructivism.

**Hypothesis:** A tentative explanation, based on previous observations and experiences that can be tested by investigations. For example, 'the Lego wall fell down because the bricks need to fit so that they overlap' and 'if I add glycerine to the washing up liquid the bubbles will be larger'.

**Instructional representations:** Whereas some psychologists talk of mental representations that learners construct for themselves as they learn, in this book we have focused on instructional representations. This means the variety of teaching materials which are used to convey to learners something about the subject, to make it easier for them to learn. The most effective forms of instructional representation are models, analogies, illustrations, drawings, explanations and demonstrations.

**Investigations:** Of all the activities which teachers offer children to learn science, investigations are unique. They involve children in making systematic changes to objects, in order to conduct a fair-test. (see variables)

**Knowledge base:** In 1986–7 Lee Shulman proposed a framework for a knowledge base for teachers. It consisted of seven categories, three of which have been of primary interest in this book. They are: subject content knowledge, (facts, concepts and the deep organising structure of the discipline and the nature of enquiry), pedagogical content knowledge, (ways of representing the subject to make it comprehensible to others) and knowledge of learners.

**Model:** Some models are three-dimensional. For example, one which shows the relationship of Earth to the Sun and Moon reduces the complexity of the solar system to a manageable form. Children can play with the model, watch its behaviour and make predictions about how the parts will function. Scientists use models in similar ways, constructing chemical structures or aerofoil sections. Other models allow scientists to play with ideas in abstract ways, working out how things function or might be, (like the wave model of light); models are often stepping stones towards a theory. Models reflect the tentative nature of science, with implications that they invite predictions which can then be tested.

**National Curriculum:** Introduced by the 1988 Education Act for schools in England and Wales. In the primary school there are three core subjects, English, maths and science, and six foundation subjects which have to be taught to children of ages 5–11. Ages 5–7 are known as *Key Stage 1* and 7–11 as *Key Stage 2*. The associated assessment system is described in a number of *Attainment Targets,* that knowledge and skills which children of different abilities are expected to have achieved. These are described in more precise detail, as *Statements of Attainment,* the basis of criterion referenced assessment.

**Procedural understanding (knowledge):** Concerned with the skills needed to conduct an investigation. These include identifying variables, designing the investigation, observing, measuring, recording, interpreting, and being critical of faulty procedures. These elements of enquiry are known as *process skills.*

**Pedagogical thinking (knowledge):** Is concerned with justifying the selection of certain teaching strategies and explanatory devices. (see instructional representations)

**Variables:** To conduct a fair test children must first understand that there are elements which affect their investigation. For example, Which is the bounciest ball? Some variables can be controlled systematically: the *independent variable* – the type of ball; *control variables* stay the same – height of drop, type of floor, etc. Other variables cannot be controlled directly: the *dependent variable* – the height of a ball's bounce. This can be measured.

# References

## Introduction

Kennedy, M. (1991) *Teaching Academic Subjects to Diverse Learners*, New York: Teachers College Press.

## Unit 1

Bennett, N. and Carré, C. (1993) *Learning to Teach*, London: Routledge.
Claxton, G. (1986) 'The alternative conceivers' conceptions', *Studies in Science Education*, 13, 123–30.
DES (1983) *Assessment of Performance Unit, Science in Schools, Age 11: Report No. 2*, London: HMSO.
DES (1988) *Assessment of Performance Unit, Science at Age 11: a Review of APU Findings 1980–84*, London: HMSO.
DES (1989 and 1991) *Science in the National Curriculum*, London: HMSO.
Harlen, W. (ed.) (1985) *Primary Science: Taking the Plunge*, London: Heinemann.
Mant, J. and Summers, M. (1993) 'Some primary school teachers' understanding of the Earth's place in the universe', *Research Papers in Education*, 8, 1, 101–29.
Shulman, L. (1986) 'Those who understand: knowledge growth in teaching', *Educational Researcher*, 15, 2, 4–14.
Stodolsky, S. S. (1988) *The Subject Matters*, Chicago: University of Chicago Press.
Symington, D. and Osborne, R. (1985) 'Towards professional development in science education for the primary school teacher', *European Journal of Science Education*, 7, 1, 19–28.
Swatton, P. (1992) 'Children's language and assessing their skill in formulating testable hypotheses', *British Educational Research Journal*, 18, 1, 73–85.

## Unit 2

Bruner, J. (1966) *Studies in Cognitive Growth*, New York: Wiley.
Bruner, J. (1974) *Beyond the Information Given*, London: Allen & Unwin.

McDiarmid, W., Ball, D. L. and Anderson, C. (1989) 'Why staying one chapter ahead doesn't really work: subject-specific pedagogy', in M. Reynolds (ed.) *Knowledge Base for the Beginning Teacher*, New York: Pergamon.

Parker, L. (1990) 'Teaching about electricity: the teacher's concept and the pupil's learning', *Education 3–13*, 18, 3, 13–19.

Reid Banks, L. (1980) *The Indian in the Cupboard*, New York: Avon Camelot.

Shulman, L. (1986) 'Those who understand: knowledge growth in teaching', *Educational Researcher*, 15, 2, 4–14.

## Unit 3

Alexander, R., Rose, J. and Woodhead, C. (1992) *Curriculum Organisation and Practice in the Primary Classroom*, London: HMSO.

Bennett, N. and Carré, C. (1993) *Learning to Teach*, London: Routledge.

Cosgrove, M. and Osborne, R. (1985) 'Lesson frameworks for changing children's ideas', in R. Osborne and P. Freyberg (eds) *Learning in Science: the Implications of 'Children's Science'*, London: Heinemann.

Driver, R. (1983) *The Pupil as Scientist?*, Milton Keynes: Open University Press.

Driver, R., Guesne, E. and Tiberghien, A. (eds) (1985) *Children's Ideas in Science*, Milton Keynes: Open University Press.

Dunne, E. and Bennett, N. (1990) *Talking and Learning in Groups*, London: Routledge.

Harlen, W. (ed.) (1985) *Taking the Plunge*, London: Heinemann.

Jelly, S. (1985) 'Helping children raise questions – and answering them', in W. Harlen (ed.) *Taking the Plunge*, London: Heinemann.

Lawson, A. (1991) 'What teachers need to know to teach science effectively', in M. Kennedy, (ed.) *Teaching Academic Subjects to Diverse Learners*, New York: Teachers College Press.

Osborne, R. (1985) 'Children's own concepts', in W. Harlen (ed.) *Taking the Plunge*, London: Heinemann.

Watts, M. (1983) 'A study of schoolchildren's alternative frameworks of the concept of force', *European Journal of Science Education*, 5, 2, 217–30, and in Hodgson, B. and Scanlon, E. (eds) (1985) *Approaching Primary Science*, London: Harper & Row.

Wittrock, M. (1974) 'Learning as a generative process', *Educational Psychology* 11, 87–95, and in Osborne, R. and Freyberg, P. (1985) *Learning in Science: the Implications of 'Children's Science'*, London: Heinemann.

## Unit 4

Claxton, G. (1991) *Educating the Enquiring Mind: the Challenge For School Science*, Hemel Hempstead: Harvester Wheatsheaf.

NCC (1991) *Science Explorations INSET*, London: NCC.

Preece, P. (1978) 'Exploration of semantic space: a review of research on the organisation of scientific concepts in semantic memory', *Science Education* 62, 4, 547–62.

Qualter, A., Strang, J., Swatton, P. and Taylor, R. (1990) *Exploration: a Way Of Learning Science*, Oxford: Blackwell.

Sutton, C. (1992) *Words, Science And Learning*, Buckingham: OU Press.

Taylor, R. (1990) 'The National Curriculum: a study to compare levels of attainment with data from the APU science surveys (1980–84)', *School Science Review*, 72, 258, 31–7.

## Unit 5

Lampert, M. (1985) 'How do teachers manage to teach? Perspectives on problems in practice', *Harvard Educational Review*, 55, 2, 178–94.

Mitchell, C. and Koshy, V. (1993) *Effective Teacher Assessment*, London: Hodder & Stoughton.

Qualter, A., Strang, J., Swatton, P. and Taylor, R. (1990) *Exploration: a Way of Learning Science*, Oxford: Blackwell.


## Unit 6

Alexander, R., Rose, J. and Woodhead, C. (1992) *Curriculum Organisation and Practice in the Primary Classroom*, London: HMSO.

Bennett, N. and Carré, C. (1993) *Learning to Teach*, London: Routledge.

Claxton, G. (1984) *Live and Learn: an Introduction to the Psychology of Growth and Change in Everyday Life*, London: Harper & Row.

Cleminson, A. (1990) 'Establishing an epistemological base for science teaching in the light of contemporary notions of the nature of science and of how children learn science', *Journal of Research in Science Teaching*, 27, 5, 429–45.

Feyerabend, P. (1975) *Against Method*, London: Verso.

Medawar, P. (1982) *Pluto's Republic*, Oxford: Oxford University Press.

Popper, K. R. (1959) *The Logic of Scientific Discovery*, London: Hutchinson.

Ryan, A. and Aikenhead, G. (1992) 'Students' preconceptions about the epistemology of science', *Science Education*, 76, 6, 559–80.

Smith, D. and Neale, D. (1991) 'The construction of subject matter knowledge in primary science teaching', in J. Brophy (ed.) *Advances in Research on Teaching: a Research Annual, Volume 2*, Greenwich, Connecticut: JAI Press.

White, R. (1988) *Learning Science*, Oxford: Blackwell.

Wolfe, L. F. (1989) 'Analyzing science lessons: a case study with gifted children', *Science Education*, 73, 1, 87–100.

Woolgar, S. (1988) *Science – the very idea*, London: Tavistock Publications.

Ziman, J. (1980) *Teaching and Learning about Science and Society*, Cambridge: Cambridge University Press.

# Index